WOMAN IN A MAN'S CHURCH

Arlene Swidler

iPub Global Connection, LLC

Published by iPub Global Connection, LLC

www.iPubCloud.com

1050 W. Nido Avenue, Mesa, AZ 85210

info@iPubCloud.com

Paperback ISBN 978-1-948575-01-0

ABOUT IPUBCLOUD.COM

You've opened the right book from the iPub international library. You might be a scholar, an avid reader, a mother or father, a teacher, a 'tween or teen, or one of the rest of us.

Welcome home to iPub Global Connection where knights of old and now digital nomads from all over the world meet safely to share ideas, find resources, and support individuals whose voices wish to be heard to create and protect the world for your great-great-grandchildren.

We are committed to the empowerment of everyone's contributions to a better world. Often, we feel paralyzed by our limiting doubt that alone we have no ability or opportunity to make any real impact. When that thought comes up, pick up the eraser in your mind's eye and say "backspace, delete." Individually, together, we can and will influence causing the important changes to ensure a habitable world for future generations....a world embracing global citizenship one by one.

How would *you* begin to define global citizenship? One way might be to remain open enough to learn about other cultures and peoples so that we can connect with all. There are, of course, many ways— through music, art, blogs, podcasts, philosophy, all of which help children model how to be better citizens.

Here you may find what you're looking for, the idea you'd like to expand...a place to be open, to learn, and to trust.

Read on and become a part of the ongoing conversations. Email a note, comment, or share your idea or blog post. Don't keep your views or us a secret. Your voice counts and we care.

This world is in dire need of love, patience, and respect and iPub Publishing is a place where you may find a sentinel in the direction to achieve this transformation. We, along with you, can be a guide towards world peace, improving communication through dialogue, advancing diplomacy among nations to engage with differences. Our international writers, authors, thinkers, and scholars are here to make you think....**Join the renaissance!**

iPub Global Connection, LLC

www.iPubCloud.com

1050 W. Nido Avenue, Mesa, AZ 85210
www.iPubCloud.com
US telephone: 484-775-0008
info@iPubCloud.com

TABLE OF CONTENTS

DEDICATION BY SANDRA BILLINGSLEA - SWIDLER

I met Arlene 61 years ago. I was 16. She and my brother, Leonard (Leo to me at that time, Len today) were dating. This was the era of Grace Kelly, the most magnificent, beautiful, poised, powerful woman in the world. (My goodness, she had married a prince.) What greater impact could there be, than these criteria. Then I met my brother's 'friend', who I was convinced must have been related to Grace Kelly. She most certainly, in my eyes, looked enough like Grace Kelly to be her sister. She had the same chiseled features. She walked with the most purposeful stride I had ever seen. She was magnificent. She was the first powerful woman I had ever met. And, she talked to me like I had an idea or two. Another first! She explained to me it was important to always have an extra toothbrush in my home for a house guest, in case someone came to visit and had forgotten theirs.

To this day, were you to come to my home, there will be a toothbrush waiting for you, just in case. Almost as important, in my 16-year-old mind, was the idea of an empowered woman. I had never heard of such a notion. Honestly, I was not quite sure what that meant. I realize today, those words and concepts became the rocks upon which I built my life. Arlene was one of a handful of women taking on the socially inappropriate world of women's rights. Even more challenging, Arlene had the audacity to suggest women have a role in the Catholic Church. This approached heresy.

I am confident when you read her book you will discover her courage and wisdom. They will support you in today's world as they have me through my life. Enjoy!

Sandi Billingslea - Swidler

FOREWORD BY LEONARD SWIDLER

Arlene Anderson Swidler was, among many things, an overlooked pioneer in "Second Wave Feminism," whose beginning usually is linked by Betty Friedan's 1963 publication of *The Feminine Mystique*. Not long afterward, in 1966, Arlene published her first article, bringing Feminism into American Catholic consciousness in *Commonweal*, the premier American Catholic periodical on public affairs: "The Male Church," (June 24, 1966). This was before either later Catholic "Feminist Stars" Rosemary Reuther or Mary Daly broke into print!

Once started, Arlene continued on a publishing roll. (Actually, already, it was her idea, shortly after we returned from several years of research and teaching in Germany, to launch the first, and premier, scholarly periodical devoted to ecumenical and interreligious dialogue: *Journal of Ecumenical Studies* (1964—). That same year she published "Feminine Mystique in a Male Church" [Address at Eastern Regional Catholic Press Assoc. Convention in Wilmington, DE], *Delmarva Dialogue*. (Nov.18, 1966). After that, she went on, at least, an annual feminist publishing spree:

"An Ecumenical Question: The Status of Women," *Journal of Ecumenical Studies* (Winter 1967). "The Forgotten Neighbor" [on ecological responsibility of religions], *Journal of Ecumenical Studies* (Fall 1967). "Women: The Church's Third Class Citizens," *American Catholic Exodus*, 1968. "Brownson and the 'Woman Question,'" *American Benedictine Review* (June, 1968). "Make Theology Your Business," *Word* [National Council of Catholic Women] (Dec. 1969). "The Hows and Why," *Word* (May, 1970).

Then, for the next several years Arlene published 14 columns in the major Catholic weekly independent newspaper, the *National Catholic Reporter* on feminist themes, including: "Can a Married Woman Have a Name that's Hers Alone?" (Apr 20, 1971). "Progress (or No Progress) Report: Academic Women's Lib," (July 2, 1971). "Symbolic Actions for Women's Lib," (Aug 27, 1971). "Catholic Liberationists: Feminists in the Middle," (Oct 22, 1971). "Men, Not Women, Control Giving," (Dec 10, 1971). "Women's Religious Witness," (Jan 14, 1972). "Protestants Make Women's Groups Go,"

(Feb 4, 1972). "Men Decide What Women Do," (Mar 24, 1972). "Stalling Tactic by Churchmen: 'Ecumenism' a Phony Argument," (May 26, 1972). "Status Problems: No 'Baby Steps' to Married Priests," (Oct 6, 1972)." Catholics Should Take Initiative: A Time for Dialogue on Abortion," (Dec 1, 1972. "The Sexist Church: Women Want Church Jobs," (1973). "Arguments Against Women: The Retreat to 'Tradition,'" (June 8, 1973). "American Feminists Not Alone," (Oct 19, 1973). "Women's Rights in the Church: Why Are Women 'Sons of God'?" (April 1, 1977). "Now We Are Three" [on Jewish-Christian-Muslim dialogue], (May 27, 1977). "Let's Have Lay Preachers Now," (Sept16, 1977). "If Deaconesses, Why Not Priests? (Nov 25, 1977). "The Founder of Catholic U Was a 21-year-old Woman," (May 20, 1988).

Altogether, Arlene published 75 articles, 26 book reviews, 7 book translations from German to English, and authored or edited 13 books, and edited a magazine, *Word*, and the *Journal of Ecumenical Studies*, taught at nine different universities in the U.S., Europe and Asia. The books she either authored or edited included: *World Religions. Concern: A Discussion Series*, 1970; *Bishops and People*, ed. with Leonard Swidler, 1970; *Woman in a Man's Church*, 1972; *Sistercelebrations. Nine Worship Experiences*, 1974; *Women Priests. A Catholic Commentary On The Vatican Declaration,* ed. with Leonard Swidler, 1976; *Judaism for Young People. A Bibliography* [annotated], ed. with Josephine Z. Knopp, 1978; *Human Rights in Religious Traditions*, ed., 1982; *Mainstreaming Feminist Research for Teaching Religious Studies*. Ed. with Walter E. Conn, 1985; *Marriage Among The Religions Of The World*, ed. 1990; *A New Phoebe. Perspectives on Roman Catholic Women and the Permanent Diaconate*, ed. with Virginia Kaib Ratigan, 1990; *Homosexuality and World Religions*, ed. 1993.

This clearly is an impressive intellectual output! She was also a brilliant lecturer and teacher—in short, a brilliant mind that could make complicated matters simple and clear—as she does in this book. Beyond all this, and in its very midst, Arlene was an impressive human person—my Jewish forebears and colleagues would say a *Mensch*!

Professor Leonard Swidler

PREFACE

For years now, we've been talking about the kind of religious book that gives us all the answers even before we've formulated the questions. Nowhere has this been more true than in the area of Catholic Womanhood. Long before our daughters were old enough to be aware that they were anything other than ordinary people we were teaching them that they had special female goals, female models, female ways of thinking, and even a special female spirituality.

Of course the adults themselves—both male and female—had been taught the same things when they were too young to doubt or protest, and the tradition goes back and back until it rests on the Bible or the Church Fathers and Doctors. Nowhere did it get a major impulse from the only legitimate source of knowledge, the feminine experience.

This book does not attempt to give new answers to the old questions; the author not only refuses to acknowledge that the right questions have been asked in the past, but she doubts that the right questions can even be formulated today. First women must be conscious of their own womanhood, and that involves a tremendous task—sorting through all the debris of thousands of years to decide what's myth and what's truth. This book is intended as a candle to help light the sorting, though if in the process some of the dead wood catches fire and burns up, the author will be pleased.

Perhaps some time in the future it will be possible for our new Catholic women— aware of themselves and where they are going—to write a new Catholic "theology of woman," but secretly I hope no one will want to bother.

Arlene Swidler 1971

1. WHAT'S A WOMAN AND WHO DECIDES?

In the beginning, according to one of the assumedly all male authors of the Bible, there was a man, Adam. This man, according to Genesis 2:20, gave the names to all the animals and birds around him. Supposedly, by classifying things and deciding what's what, the man gained control over the rest of creation.

Something like that has gone on in the man-woman relationship almost ever since. The male has done the classifying, the organizing, and the writing; the female has been the subject of philosophizing, theologizing, psychologizing, and sometimes just daydreaming.

So even today if you want to know what a woman is, you'll pretty well have to get a man's opinion. The books in the library are mostly written by men. The psychiatrists who tell us what's right or wrong with women are mostly men—and men accustomed to dealing with a special group of women at that. The churches which decide what a woman should become are all completely male-dominated. What's a woman? "Ask a man," seems to be our civilization's answer.

Much of the theorizing has been done in a vacuum. This is most especially true in the religious area, for where women are concerned, what could be more of a vacuum than a monastery? And that, of course, is where Thomas Aquinas worked. He entered at the age of five. It is from Aquinas that many of our Catholic ideas on women come, for Thomas is to this day the preeminently official theologian and philosopher of the Church.

Thomas' big contribution to Catholic thought was his enormous synthesis of traditional Christian thought and ancient Greek philosophy and science in his *Summa Theologica*. His ideas on women thus combine the attitudes of the Church Fathers and the theories of Aristotle; both strains are misogynist.

Aristotle was a biologist, but facts known in the fourth century before Christ were few. Instead, men and women got pushed into the philosophical categories of form and matter.

These ideas were taken over by Thomas.

1

According to Thomas, there is only one thing for which women are necessary, only one area in which men cannot be better helped by another man. That of course is procreation. The idea that there is only one thing that women need men for would never have occurred to him.

But even in procreation Thomas sees the woman playing a very inferior role. Using the Aristotelian categories of matter and form, Thomas equates the male contribution with form and the female with matter. The best analogy is with the growth of plants. The male role is like the seed, the female like the earth. The female simply nourishes what the male has planted, a concept which is understandable in a society where biological sciences are primitive. On the other hand, one wonders why looking around them didn't convince these thinkers that children were just as likely to look like (have the form of) their mothers as their fathers.

The logical conclusion of this matter-form system of thought is that the child should resemble only the father, just as the plant resembles the parent from which the seed came; to the extent it resembles the mother, the earth, it is defective. And Thomas carried this to its conclusion by labeling women "misbegotten males."

In many ways the earlier Fathers of the Church had been even more demeaning in their attitude towards women. Tertullian is famous for his statement to women, "You are the devil's gateway." According to Epiphanius, "Woman is easily seducible, weak, and without great understanding." Both of these men were clearly drawing their conclusions from what they had read in the Bible.

This is the way women have been regarded throughout history. Most women have been mothers and housewives and confined completely or at least to a much greater extent than their men. It has been the men who met with one another, did the talking and the philosophizing and the organizing. The system has always—at least in the historical reaches of our own past—been a male system. The male has been the norm, the human being. The female has been "different," peripheral.

Of course, there have been rebellious uppity women in the Church who tried to do their own thing, and there have been men who tried to help them. Women in religious orders who wanted to *do* something rather than simply *be* something—who saw their destiny as active collaborators in Christ's mission rather than merely the object of male pastoral care—have existed through the centuries.

Mary Ward, the founder of the "English Ladies" in the seventeenth century, is a famous example. Her idea was to have a group of women religious, living outside a cloister without a distinctive habit, who would be under the direction of a woman superior general with authority to transfer them as they were needed. These "English Ladies" would devote themselves to teaching girls and giving them a solid academic grounding, including such masculine subjects as Latin.

But her order, like the Jesuits she had to some extent modeled the group on, was suppressed by Pope Urban VIII. His Papal Bull stated that the group among other things was trying to carry out works "by no means suiting the weakness of their sex." Mary Ward herself, not convinced the Bull was authentic, tried to continue her work and was actually imprisoned by members of the Holy Office in a convent in Munich.

The Visitation nuns, now one of the more strict and less experimental groups, began as a contemplative but uncloistered congregation designed to visit the sick poor in their own homes. But after only a few years the women were forced by the hierarchy to become a religious order with strict enclosure. Nowadays they don't do much visiting.

Today Sisters are rethinking what it means to be a woman religious, often with dynamic results. Yet in the universal church, and very often in individual dioceses, men still think they must define the role.

Secular culture has not been any less male-dominated. When you think about it, all the outstanding women personalities in literature up until almost the present have been male inventions. Medea and Antigone of the ancient Greek plays, Dido of the Aeneid, Juliet, Desdemona, Lady Macbeth and today's Liza Doolittle and Olive Oyl—all are inventions of the masculine mind. Down through all these centuries people have been learning about human nature through studying a male-dominated literature.

Even today, when we have a number of first-rate women novelists, lots of men try to avoid reading what they think of as "women's books." Occasional college men complain to their literature professors if they are assigned novels by or about women.

One of the more obvious ways to see how our young people today—both boys and girls are being taught their sex roles is to look at their textbooks. Studies of school materials have been made in the past by groups dedicated to interracial and interreligious understanding, and now within the past few years feminist groups have been using the same techniques.

Everything from literature to history can be examined for its references or lack of references to women. Even things like mathematics books are scrutinized. Are there more problems and illustrations about Johnny than Mary? And is Johnny doing more interesting things than Mary? Is he shown calculating the amount of fuel for a trip to Mars while she doubles the recipe for gingerbread?

Most recently church groups have been checking their own publications for possible sex discrimination, and of course they have been finding it in great quantity. The Methodists seem to have been the first to publish a full-scale study, in this case of their own Sunday School curricula.

In the third and fourth grade levels, the Methodist committee found, among other things, that there are 54 pictures of boys in the student book and 29 of females. Though the Methodist Church has ordained women for many years, all of the ministers and missionaries portrayed in the curriculum are males, and the idea of such a vocation for girls is discouraged in one story by ridicule.

Women are seldom mentioned in occupational terms, the report says, and married women are never identified as working outside the home. Women are portrayed as doing housework in 13 instances, but no men are.

In some ways the findings of the Methodist team in their review of the nursery school curriculum were even more important. The materials for three-year-olds were found to be full of sex-stereotyping. Besides the occupational stereotyping and the homebody mother image of the third and fourth grade level, the committee presented statistics like these:

a) Girls appearing as those who are passive, powerless, waiting on others, needing help and protection, watching the action, unhappy: [Twenty Eight]

b) Girls as active in play activities: [Five]

c) Boys appearing as active, brave, protectors of women, angry, playing with blocks, trucks, etc., in control: [Thirty one]

d) Boys reading or in some other passive activity: [Three]

Typical examples:

> "Clink, clink. Brad put his money in the basket on the beauty center. The teacher helped Wendy open her purse so she could get her money out."

> "The farmer gave the children a special treat. He let each one of them pick a pumpkin, any one they liked. Brian pulled his from the vine all by himself. Missy needed the teacher to help with hers."

One of the most peculiarly American aspects of the contemporary feminine image is that of "consumer." The man—so the argument runs—is expected to produce, the woman is supposed to consume. Thorstein Veblen, an American economist writing his book *The Theory of the Leisure Class* at the end of the last century, coined two phrases that sum up the consumer concept rather neatly: "conspicuous consumption" and "conspicuous leisure."

Veblen's idea was that in order to have status one must not merely have wealth, one must display this wealth. One way is by "conspicuous abstention from labor." Such conspicuous leisure does not mean idleness, but merely being active in a non-productive way (he included religion and sports among his list of nonproductive occupations). The second way of impressing people was by "conspicuous consumption." Veblen thought this function of the leisure class was so well established that not to eat well, dress well and live in a tastefully furnished house marked a man of our society as inferior.

Already in the last century Veblen noted that the wife was expected to be a vicarious consumer for the head of the household—he points out the deliberately impractical bonnets and high heels of the lady which show she is incapable of productive work, and even adds,

5

"The substantial reason for our tenacious attachment to the skirt is just this: it is expensive and it hampers the wearer at every turn and incapacitates her for all useful exertion."

The woman as vicarious conspicuous consumer is at least as much with us today as she was then. Where a woman of not too many years ago was respected for cooking and sewing well, today's woman is a source of pride to her husband if she knows the smart artists to patronize, the "in" designers, the chic resort to visit. That's the image the mass media are trying to project.

In the middle classes the emphasis is more on home furnishings and gourmet cookery, and while' retaining her position as consumer the wife becomes more of a drudge, spending more and more time in housework. (This doesn't promote or demote her to the producer class simply because the work of cooking up exotic meals or polishing the furniture with special waxes is essentially useless.)

Betty Friedan argued this same point of view in her book *The Feminine Mystique*, which appeared in 1963 and is credited with starting the whole new women's rights movement. Friedan, herself a free-lance writer for women's magazines for a number of years, had long been interested in the growing unhappiness of so many women who were trying to conform to the happy housewife image. One of the major influences was the new image which the women's magazines started presenting in the late 'forties. Heroines in earlier issues had usually lived their own lives, had their own independent thoughts they even took flying lessons on the sly, or put their jobs before a date.

Then suddenly, in the late 'forties, there was a shift to stories and features about women who did nothing outside of the home and family. The reason, Friedan finally learned, is that at the end of the war the men returned and slowly took over the jobs as writers and editors for. the women's magazines. And these men yearned for the comfort of a home after the days on the battlefield.

What cinched the change, according to Friedan, was the fact that these women's home magazines know they can sell more of their product—sewing machines, laundry soaps, appliances of various types—to the woman who stays at home and thinks of herself as a "professional" homemaker. It made good sense to make the women proud of their roles as consumers.

In some ways working women are made to play the consumer game even more dramatically. How many times a woman is hired on the basis of her appearance! A receptionist or secretary is more and more often expected to dress in the latest fashion to add glory to the boss's reputation. "This firm wants to look like it's going places. We need people who reflect that in the front office."

So what do all these images add up to? There is no doubt that women come out as second best. Women are sort of handy assistants in the usual image: assistants merely in procreation, according to one view, or in more general ways in today's world—the typist to the executive, the nurse to the doctor, the checker to the supermarket manager. Women appear as not terribly bright, not very ambitious, slightly silly, likely to worry over their hair-dos, and eager to please the male of the species. Watch your local television station for details.

It's equally clear that the image has been put together over the centuries by men, sometimes consciously, sometimes not, and that the image is very helpful to men in many ways: it bolsters the ego, it gives men more leisure, it keeps women out of the power structure.

One of the first things we need today is the free atmosphere in which women can decide for themselves just what they are and what they are intended to be. One of the more interesting parallels between women and Blacks as oppressed groups is the way each has been stereotyped in the past—as somewhat irresponsible, uncritical, perfectly content with a secondary role, emotional—as all the things which helped the white male keep his status. In the past both groups have for the most part accepted the stereotypes and made them their own. Today the Blacks are rebelling, and the women are only a few years behind.

But after a woman has been brought up from her infancy with special feminine toys, feminine clothes, feminine ways of getting approval, and feminine ways of earning a living, she can't decide one day that tomorrow she will be her real self. She can't differentiate between what she really wants and what she has been taught to want.

We will need women psychologists and psychiatrists speaking and writing from their own personal and professional experience, women marriage counselors in larger numbers, more women sociologists and women college presidents before women will be free enough from male pressures to think about themselves objectively. (Let's hope that they won't then decide to write books of philosophy and theology about what it means to be male!)

More and more women are insisting that the male-female relation discussion must be a dialogue. The time is past when Whites could tell Blacks what they were and what they ought to be and how they ought to react to things or what the Black experience was. In the ecumenical arena one of the first rules is to let each side define itself, present its own views, and choose its own leaders. Why not take women seriously too?

This is especially true in the question of psychological differences. Are men and women born with different values and tendencies or do they learn them? In the past almost everyone has insisted quite strongly that men and women are different, or rather that *women* are different. Men are never the different ones; they have always been the standard, and women are the Other, the different ones. Men have enjoyed developing the idea.

Yet our culture is very strongly male-dominated; what we know about being human comes from male philosophers, theologians, psychologists and historians. It should then be up to women to say whether their own experience is different from this widely-known norm. A man can neither know from experience what it means to be feminine nor compare his own masculine experience with knowledge in the form of a tradition of female-authored literature, art, philosophy, and history—there simply isn't any.

This is the reason for the female consciousness groups springing up around the country, more and more often within Christian church structures. Here women can get together and discover how much they have in common what it means to be female in America three-fourths through the twentieth century.

And after self-definition we'll be ready for dialogue.

The second big need of today—and this is especially notable within the Church—is the need to force ourselves to get along without female stereotypes. Men are extremely fortunate not to have all those books written about them. All those definitions have set limits and narrowed options. So what we need are not new theologies of women or even sex, for they would only bring new stereotypes. Many, many women in the church and society say they are happy living in their traditional ways. Many others feel that their talents and humanity are being stifled. Stereotyping looks at these two female self-images and says, "Woman is either ... or ...... Liberation in Christ Jesus says, "Women are both."

A famous English novelist described in 1928her reactions to the evening paper.

"Some previous luncher had left the lunch edition of the evening paper on a chair, and, waiting to be served, I began idly reading the headlines. A ribbon of very large letters ran across the page. Somebody had made a big score in South Africa. Lesser ribbons announced that Sir Austen Chamberlain was at Geneva. A meat axe with human hair on it had been found in a cellar. Mr. Justice commented in the Divorce Courts upon the Shamelessness of Women. Sprinkled about the paper were other pieces of news. A film actress had been lowered from a peak in California and hung suspended in mid-air. The weather was going to be foggy. The most transient visitor to this planet, I thought, who picked up this paper could not fail to be aware, even from this scattered testimony, that England is under the rule of a patriarchy. Nobody in their senses could fail to detect the dominance of the professor (her symbol for the male who writes books about females). His was the power and the money and the influence. He was the proprietor of the paper and its editor and sub-editor. He was the Foreign Secretary and the Judge. He was the cricketer; he owned the race-horses and the yachts. He was the director of the company that pays two hundred per cent to its shareholders. He left millions to charities and colleges that were ruled by himself. He suspended the film actress in mid-air. He will decide if the hair on the meat axe is human; he it is who will acquit or convict the murderer, and hang him, or let him go free. With the exception of the fog he seemed to control everything." (Virginia Woolf, *A Room of One's Own*, New York, 1929)

Look over last night's paper. How much have things changed?

Compare your city newspaper with your diocesan paper.

Jot down the items in the evening's TV news coverage. What impression of the role of women would a foreign visitor get?

A New Jersey minister, Rev. Dr. Thomas Boslooper, spent ten years on a study of successful women, interviewing 300 "women of accomplishment" and 150 husbands. His conclusion: All mature, intellectually creative women were tomboys when they were young. Among his other findings:

"Successful women with severe emotional problems get little or no physical exercise.

"The more physically active a woman is, the closer her intellectual capacities come to a man's.

"Many physically active women try to keep their athletic prowess hidden because society tends to regard the woman athlete as unfeminine." (The New York Times, Dec. 27,1967)

Do his findings parallel your own experiences?

What pressures militate against women's being athletes?

Compare the encouragement and financial support given boy and girl athletes in the school systems.

Do church and other youth organizations tend to favor the male athlete?

To what extent do women help form the contemporary image of women? Check the following:

The number and professional status of women employed by the major news magazines.

The extent to which men direct women's fashion and homemaking magazines check the mastheads.

The employment of women by the major men's magazines.

The writers and producers of popular television programs.

2. WOMAN IN A MAN'S BOOK

Hardly anybody today—either Christian or Jewish—can get very enthusiastic about a lecture or book on Women in the Bible. We don't expect anything useful or pertinent to the twentieth century, and we usually discover our expectations were correct. Very few of the women presented in the Old Testament can serve as models to an independent woman today. There are the romantic stories of Susanna, Bath-Sheba, Delilah, and even Queen Esther, all of whom assumed importance simply because of their connection of one sort or another with men, and all of whom won this attention because of their physical beauty.

Women of a different sort—Deborah the Judge, for example—are not displayed for our Christian edification very often, and, in fact, are not given much visibility in the Bible itself. Deborah, "who used to sit under Deborah's Palm between Ramah and Bethel in the highlands of Ephraim, and the Israelites would come to her to have their disputes decided," is a much less developed literary personality than her contemporary, Ruth.

Ruth is perhaps the Old Testament woman most often held up as a model. A whole book, albeit a very short one, is devoted to the story of this 'Moabite woman who, when widowed, decided to accompany her widowed mother-in-law Naomi back to Naomi's home in Jerusalem. There, through her industry and intelligence, she finds a kinsman, Boaz, to marry her and thus legally continue her first husband's family line. Certainly there are worthwhile lessons to be drawn from the story—respect and love for one's mother-in-law not the least—but basically Ruth is the epitome of the religious stereotype of the Good Woman; she is passive, hardworking, obedient, apparently unconcerned about greater issues. Perhaps this is why the passage proves popular at Catholic weddings.

There is one Old Testament passage, at the conclusion of the Book of Proverbs, which is often quoted as honoring women. It's the description of the "valiant woman," or, in one of the newer translations, the "perfect wife." Here is a woman who accomplishes things, runs her household well, is admired by men. "She does her work with eager hands." "She sets her mind on a field, then she buys it; with what her hands have earned she plants a vineyard ... .. She weaves linen sheets and sells them, she supplies the merchant with sashes." The passage concludes,

Charm is deceitful, and beauty empty; the woman who is wise is the one to praise.

Give her a share in what her hands have worked for, and let her works tell her praises at the city gates.

Each Friday night as the Sabbath begins, the Jewish family gathers at the dinner table for blessings and the recitation of this passage by the husband. The ritual is often cited by Jews as an illustration of the respect Judaism shows its women, but some contemporary Jewish women are not impressed. As one of them said, "Just look at the opening line of the passage. 'A perfect wife—who can find her?'"

We don't have to be Bible scholars to analyze and evaluate the most-often quoted New Testament texts referring to the position of women in Christianity. In one adult education class on sexuality, we decided on the spur of the moment to dispense with a lecture on the Biblical texts and just reproduce the important passages and let the group do its own analysis.

Our hunch was right. A good discussion got everyone thinking and we came up with almost all the important conclusions the scholars have been talking about. Here are the texts we used.

I Cor. 11, 7-16:

A man should certainly not cover his head, since he is the image of God and reflects God's glory; but woman is the reflection of man's glory. For man did not come from woman; no, woman came from man; and man was not created for the sake of woman, but woman was created for the sake of man. That is the argument for women's covering their heads with a symbol of the authority over them....

Ask yourselves if it is fitting for a woman to pray to God without a veil; and whether nature itself does not tell you that long hair on a man is nothing to be admired, while a woman, who was given her hair as a covering, thinks long hair her glory?

To anyone who might still want to argue: it is not the custom with us, nor in the churches of God.

I Cor. 14, 26-35:

So, my dear brothers, what conclusion is to be drawn? At all your meetings, let everyone be ready with a psalm or a sermon or a revelation, or ready to use his gift of tongues or to give an interpretation; but it must always be for the common good. If there are people present with the gift of tongues, let only two or three, at the most, be allowed to use it, and only one at a time, and there must be someone to interpret. If there is no interpreter present, they must keep quiet in church and speak only to themselves and to God. As for prophets, let two or three of them speak, and the others attend to them. If one of the listeners receives a revelation, then the man who is already speaking should stop. For you can all prophesy in turn, so that everyone will learn something and everybody will be encouraged. Prophets can always control their prophetic spirits, since God is not a God of disorder but of peace.

As in all the churches of the saints, women are to remain quiet at meetings since they have no permission to speak; they must keep in the background as the Law itself lays it down. If they have any questions to ask, they should ask their husbands at home: it does not seem right for a woman to raise her voice at meetings.

I Tim. 2, 9-14:

Similarly, I direct that women are to wear suitable clothes and to be dressed quietly and modestly, without braided hair or gold and jewelry or expensive clothes; their adornment is to do the sort of good works that are proper for women who profess to be religious. During instruction, a woman should be quiet and respectful. I am not giving permission for a woman to teach or to tell a man what to do. A woman ought not to speak, because Adam was formed first and Eve afterwards, and it was not Adam who was led astray but the woman who was led astray and fell into sin.

First of all, our people noticed that the passages were not consistent. Scholars today sometimes suggest that the second passage from I Cor. is an interpolation from the Letter to Timothy, and the internal discrepancy is then understandable. In any case it is clear that there is no overall agreement in the theory and practice in the New

13

Testament itself, and it follows that there is no natural or moral law involved.

The first selection rules that women are to cover their heads when they pray aloud or prophesy; the second says that women are not to pray or prophesy aloud in the service at all . 1. The third goes even farther and forbids women to teach or tell men what to do. Obviously the early Christian communities differed among themselves on the question.

Secondly, the reasons for the varying rules are about the same. Paul does present some other ideas in the first selection. He obviously believes it's in the nature of things that men should keep their hair short and finally, in a note of exasperation, says, "Look, this is the way it is."

But aside from these, each of the three passages refers back to the Old Testament. In I Cor. 11 the reason given for the ruling is that woman was created from and for the sake of man. In I Tim. we read that a woman ought not to speak because Adam was created first and Eve sinned first. This takes us all the way back to Genesis, the first book of the Bible. The third passage refers to the Law, another word for Torah, or the first five books of the Bible.

There are two versions of creation in the Bible, now generally agreed to come from two different sources. The first version, in the first chapter of Genesis, is the more theological. There we read, "God created man in the image of himself, in the image of God he created him, male and female he created them."

In the second chapter of Genesis (which was actually written earlier than the first chapter) we find the whole Adam and Eve story, which most people now take as a "myth" or poetic way of explaining theological truths—in this case the teachings of the fatherhood of God and the fact that we are all one family. In this second chapter we read that Eve was created from Adam's rib.

Our class also discovered that there are many aspects of this second creation story we cannot accept literally. Yahweh-God fashioned man from dust before he caused to spring up from the soil every kind of tree, and only later did he fashion all the wild beasts and all the birds of heaven, and last of all woman.

Yet St. Paul here uses only the second version of creation in Genesis. And unless we can accept the whole second story literally, we have no basis left within the Epistles themselves for believing the sections on women are anything more than customs.

Thirdly, we all agreed that when these statements on women are seen in context they are much less impressive. In I Cor. 14 the entire passage consists of rules to preserve order. But how many are followed today? What would a pastor do if everyone—or even every male—were ready with a psalm or a sermon or a revelation at Sunday Mass? And what priest who refuses to allow women lectors on the basis of I Tim. would station someone at the door to forbid women with braided hair or gold to enter?

Yet all these rules are presented as equals in the Bible. Why have we decided to keep some and ignore others?

Another interesting point is that, although these passages are used to bar women from the priesthood, they really deal only with women speaking out in the church, and nothing more. And on this particular issue the Church has already changed her practice, allowing women lectors and commentators.

But what impressed us most is the fact that in none of these passages, nor in any dealing with the male-dominated family structure, is there any reference to the teachings and practice of Jesus.

3. JESUS

Actually, Jesus' attitude toward women was completely unlike Paul's or the strong tradition of the Old Testament. And it's quite unlike the general attitude today. Jesus, in this matter like so many others, was unique.

Over the centuries Christians, and most especially Catholics, have taken the attitude that Jesus is the model for men and Mary is the ideal for women. There is comparatively little about Mary in the Bible, and the promoters of Marian piety for women usually have in mind an image of a passive listener ("Be it done unto me according to thy word"—a beautiful example of the feminine mystique were it not that this is not a woman responding to a man but a human responding to God) and the silent, awed, eager follower of the Lord. (This conveniently ignores the story in Mark 3 that "When his relatives [his mother and brothers] heard of this, they set out to take charge of him, convinced he was out of his mind.")

The way of salvation Jesus had in mind for women was not essentially different than that for men. He was grateful to women who ministered to him—cooking, for example—but he recognized their particularly womanly work as a necessary part of life and not in itself a goal.

The story of Martha and Mary is a good example. As Luke tells us (10, 38-42):

"In the course of their journey he came to a village, and a woman named Martha welcomed him into her house. She had a sister called Mary, who sat down at the Lord's feet and listened to him speaking. Now Martha who was distracted with all the serving said, 'Lord do you not care that my sister is leaving me to do the serving all by myself? Please tell her to help me.' But the Lord answered: 'Martha, Martha,' he said 'you worry and fret about so many things, and yet few are needed, indeed only one. It is Mary who has chosen the better part; it is not to be taken from her."

It's very easy to sympathize with Martha. The house has a special guest and she wants to make the occasion itself special. She rushes around to attend to details and see that everything is done properly.

17

The situation is hectic she is "distracted," Luke says—and young sister Mary relaxes with the guests. Martha is probably mumbling to herself, "Who does she think she is the Queen of Sheba?" She certainly must have been almost beside herself to draw everyone's attention to her own inability to cope by complaining about her sister to the chief honored guest.

Jesus is sympathetic and calming. But his message is that all this housewifery and gracious-'hostessing' are not "needed." Perhaps all the hustle and bustle was a distraction to Jesus and his followers as well as to Martha herself. Jesus declares that it is the interior life, the life of the spirit and the mind that matters. Mary knows this; she has chosen the better part, and Jesus will not tell her to regress. Although Martha is left free to pursue the traditionally feminine goals, Jesus rejects her attempt to force another woman to conform. Not all Christians today would follow his lead in setting female priorities.

Luke tells another story in the next chapter.

"Now as he was speaking, a woman in the crowd raised her voice and said, 'Happy the womb that bore you and the breasts you sucked!' But he replied, 'Still happier those who hear the word of God and keep it!' "

As in the story of Martha and Mary, Jesus looks rather ungrateful at first glance. Again a woman is trying to please him, to respond to her awareness of his greatness, in a way typically feminine. Even today kindly women will say to a young man—less often to a young woman—who has achieved a goal, "My, your mother must be proud of you!"

But Jesus will have none of this. Although it must have been embarrassing for the woman, and Jesus was always careful to protect the oppressed, including women, he nevertheless felt he must correct her. His message is that people, both men and women, are to be valued according as they hear the word of God and keep it. No mother of the year in his scheme of things!

In Mark 3, when Jesus' mother and brothers arrived at his home and asked for him, he looked around at those sitting in a circle about him and said, "Here are my mother and my brothers. Anyone who does the will of God, that person is my brother and sister and mother." He made no distinction between men and women; they all gathered around him and worked toward the same goals.

Occasionally Jesus used women to carry his message—to teach and instruct in the real sense—to men as well as women. Despite all Paul's orders to the contrary, the early Church found these women emissaries so credible that there sprang up a tradition that Martha and Mary became apostles to Provence.

The first example we might draw would be the story of Jesus visiting with the Samaritan woman at the well. (John 4, 5-42.) This in itself is surprising. The woman asks, "What? You are a Jew and you ask me, a Samaritan, for a drink?" and John tells us a bit later, "At this point the disciples returned, and were surprised to find him speaking to a woman."

Jesus reveals himself to her as the Messiah, and she hurries back into the village to tell the people. There is a big turnout, and John says, "Many Samaritans of that town had believed in him on the strength of the woman's testimony."

All four of the Gospels tell us that it was women who first discovered the empty tomb, and Matthew and Mark relate that the women were then commissioned by the angels to tell the disciples. Matthew tells us that on the way from the tomb they met Jesus himself. Jesus says, "Do not be afraid; go and tell my brothers that they must leave for Galilee; they Will see me there."

There is no doubt that Jesus expected women as well as men to work toward the building up of the Christian community and to spread the Good News.

Christianity is not alone in moving from a more enlightened attitude of its founder to a more oppressive and literal legalism in its later adherents. Islam is another good example; it makes a good parallel because both Christianity and Islam—unlike Judaism and Hinduism, for example—were founded by a single man whose teachings— unlike those of the Buddha—were written down within a generation of his own life.

Christians like to think that the condition of women in Islam is immensely inferior to that in Christianity. Catholics especially have been brought up to believe that the Church has been responsible for most of the good things that have happened to women in the last two thousand years, though recent study and even facts have proved embarrassing. The Hindus and the Jews, both supposedly terribly benighted, have each a woman as prime minister, whereas when the West German government appointed an experienced career diplomat as its representative to the Vatican she was refused accreditation on the grounds that she was a woman.

Islam is supposedly the worst of all in its treatment of women, and the veil becomes the symbol of female subjection. But the fact is that the veil comes not from Mohammad's day but some time later, and that it was borrowed from Christianity.

A contemporary Muslim woman scholar points out that the Koran granted many rights to women, including the right to choose her own husband, to earn a living, to conduct business without the consent or even the knowledge of her husband or father, to retain her own maiden name. Things have moved downhill since the time of Mohammad, but such liberated thinking is amazing for the seventh century. Women in America today [1971] are, in some states, legally forbidden to go into business without the written consent of their husbands, and use of one's own name, even where it is legally permissible in this country, can be made virtually impossible by bankers and businessmen. Our contemporary Christian culture has little to feel superior about where women are concerned.

Below are two views of the Old Testament. Do they conflict?

Which do you agree with?

Compare them with contemporary Christianity.

1) "The motivation for male domination over the female is intimately connected with the idea of paternity.... Power and property can be passed down through his sons and so clutched beyond the grave.... The male seed is of tremendous importance in the Old Testament, lines of male descent are recorded in great detail, generation by generation, and the woman is no more than a bearer of male children. . . . Since woman's only function was procreation, the greatest curse possible was for her to be barren, and the greatest favor that Jehovah could bestow on her was to make her unexpectedly fruitful in her old age, as he did Sarah and Rachel." (Eva Figes, *Patriarchal Attitudes*, Stein and Day, 1970, pp. 38-41.)

20

" 'Marriage, I think,' asserts Philip Wylie, exists primarily for the procreation of children. . . . Kids are humanity's main reason for existing.' Even God was less patriarchal; according to His own statements, He made Eve primarily to keep Adam from being lonely ('It is not good that the man should be alone; I will make him an help meet for him.')." (Morton M. Hunt, *Her Infinite Variety* Harper & Row, 1962, pp. 173-4.)

2) "in many ways Jesus strove to communicate the notion of the equal dignity of women. In one sense that effort was capped by his parable of the woman who found the lost coin (Lk. 15:8 ff.), for here Jesus projected God in the image of a woman! Luke recorded that the despised tax-collectors and sinners were gathering around Jesus, and consequently the Pharisees and scribes complained. Jesus, therefore, related three parables in a row, all of which depicted God's being deeply concerned for that which was lost. The first story was of the shepherd who left the ninety-nine sheep to seek the one lost— the shepherd is God. The third parable is of the prodigal son—the father is God. The second story is of the woman who sought the lost coin—the woman is God! Jesus did not shrink from the notion of God as feminine." (Leonard Swidler, "Jesus Was a Feminist," *Catholic World*, Jan. 1971, p. 183. iPubCloud.com)

What do the images of God the Father and God the Mother suggest?

What is your personal reaction to the Christian Science form of prayer, "God, Our Father and Mother..."?

What are the advantages and disadvantages of referring to God as Father and/or Mother?

How literally do children take the Fatherhood of God?

A Lebanese professor of Arabic Literature and Language writes that it is not Islam but Arab social customs which restrict women. She writes about woman in the Koran:

"1. God created man, both male and female. There is no clue that He created one before the other. He made them equal in creating them without distinction as to priority.

2. The Koran removed the insult that was attached to the female and the primal sin that blemished her in the story of creation. She was made equal to man, as both of them were tempted by the devil and each of them wronged himself. There is no reference to the fact that Eve tempted Adam or that she was the initiator of the temptation." (Thurayya A.F. Malhas, "The Moslem Arab Woman and Her Rights," WORD Nov. 1971, p. 3.)

How important is Eve in our attitude toward women?

How would the Moslem attitude toward women differ from ours?

How many people take the second creation story literally? How many know that there are two creation stories?

4. PRAY, SISTERS AND BROTHERS

Worship involves offering something special to God—the first fruits of the earth, an unblemished heart, a pure Victim. To the traditional mind the very word suggests descriptions like order, perfection, cleanliness, purity.

The word sex has too often suggested the opposite to religious minds—unpredictability, the irrational, and a kind of general messiness. As a result the two have been separated. And as women have had the menstrual periods, the babies, and the postpartum drainage, they have been the ones made to personify sex and impurity.

The ancient Jews had strong laws on uncleanliness. "When a woman has a discharge of blood, and blood flows from her body, this uncleanness of her monthly periods shall last for seven days (after cessation). Anyone who touches her will be unclean until evening. Any bed she lies on in this state will be unclean; any seat she sits on will be unclean. Anyone who touches her bed must wash his clothing and wash himself and will be unclean until evening" and so on (Lev. 15, 19-21). St. Matthew tells us that after the birth of Jesus his mother went to the temple to be purified.

Jesus himself apparently rejected this idea of ritual impurity. Luke, among others, tells of the woman who had had a discharge for twelve years. The self-image of that poor creature living under the taboo of Leviticus must have been almost unbearable. No wonder she tried to avoid any attention and merely touched the Master's cloak. Jesus however insisted on calling attention to her case, cured her, and went on his way with no indication of displeasure at having been made unclean!

Unfortunately, later Christians returned to the idea of menstrual uncleanness, and women were not only forbidden to say Mass but also kept a certain safe distance from the altar (the distance is much smaller today, but it's still there) and prohibited from touching the sacred vessels. When the laity were permitted to receive the consecrated bread in their hands, women had to cover their hands with a white cloth. Menstruating women were sometimes directed or urged to stay away from worship services. These taboos still exist more strongly in the Orthodox traditions than in Western Christianity, though in 1965 a Swiss lawyer wrote, "In hospitals run by religious even now some Sisters refuse to touch women during or after childbirth."

This sort of feeling against having women involved at all in the liturgy exists at such a deep-down irrational level that it's pretty difficult to argue over. It's also considerably less prevalent today than it used to be, and even those people who still believe in ritual uncleanness hesitate to bring the subject up.

What's more likely to be expressed is a feeling that it just isn't right for women to be up there in the sanctuary—and often the attitude is just that vague. Sometimes there's talk of men being more dignified (though women would certainly look at least as dignified in liturgical garments as men do) or authoritative. "Authoritative" probably comes the closest to representing the problem in the contemporary traditional mind.

In parishes where the liturgy is cool, impersonal, formal, and very traditional there is less likely to be much participation by women. And there is very likely to be a concept of the priest as the ruler, the authority figure, the spiritual patriarch. In this kind of outlook authority resides only in the Father, never the Mother.

In other situations, where the Mass is seen as a gathering together of the Christian community in love, women seem naturally to be taking on new roles. This fits in with the traditional emphasis on the liturgy as a teaching device. If our being together in Christ is to teach us the unity of his Body, we must all function together without jealousy, pride or competitiveness. Each of us has a gift, or competency, and each must use it for our common good.

So we find women beginning to act as ushers, lectors, commentators, instrumentalists, leaders of song, extraordinary ministers of the Eucharist, and even occasionally as preachers—but never as acolytes. Women need no longer be silent in the Church, but there's still the ancient fear of pollution.

The noted liturgist Father Joseph Champlin suggests that there are even more important tasks for women. He is a strong advocate of parish worship committees, which he hopes will eventually plan every Sunday worship service, with special plans for each separate Mass perhaps one with organ, one with contemporary music, one without music, etc. Such parish committees would plan themes, music, readings, commentaries, prayers of the faithful, and even suggest sermon topics and keep the congregation informed via the parish bulletin.

All of these roles and the work of a parish worship committee add up to a lot of participation for women, and in most cases they would also mean a substantial increase of male lay participation as well. But most of these things are merely talked about. A study made in 1970 by the National Council of Catholic Women came up with disappointing results.

The NCCW had set up a task force to investigate the possibilities for women to participate in the liturgy with the purpose of making suggestions to the American bishops of creative opportunities for a wider scope for women. After sending out copies of one questionnaire to every diocese in the country and copies of a second questionnaire to hundreds of parishes where the NCCW had affiliated groups, the task force discovered that women—or parishes, to be exact, were not making use of the opportunities for participation which do exist. And so the task was discovered not to be primarily the education of the bishops—although they still need consciousness raising too—but education of the parish priests and laity.

Even the diocesan liturgical commissions, usually heavily clerical and made up of establishment types, were found in many ways to be more open to women's participation than were the parish liturgy committees. Very often the local levels responded that they did not use women in the liturgy because they were following the laws of the Church, when in fact the negative laws did not exist or had been changed.

This suggested that there had not been enough interest on the local parish level to prompt inquiries or requests to the diocesan or even the national level, where some of these ideas would have been corrected. Not many of the parish committees had even discussed the question of women's participation, and the questionnaires on the diocesan level showed that when diocesan commissions had discussed the question it had been introduced by women 5 times and men 17 times.

The NCCW results must be seen in context: the laity in general has not been jumping up to volunteer with enthusiasm, for example; and even in the short time since the survey was made women's attitude toward themselves has changed. Nevertheless it's clear that women are reluctant to push themselves or even their fellow females into the liturgy.

The days of the very formal liturgy, with the priest talking Latin with his back to the people and the visible wall between the priest's area and the people's area, are not so far in the past that even very young adults cannot remember them quite clearly. Some of the same formal feeling, though without the Latin and the altar to the wall, is still prevalent in many churches today. The whole mood was deliberately arranged to represent timelessness and changelessness. People who lived and worshiped in that environment for many years were understandably shaken by innovations. Yet the introduction of lay men into the service has taken place without much ado, and it is now only lay women who for the most part must remain silent and anonymous members of the worshiping community.

Here is one of the most disconcerting and one of the most insulting problems for Catholic women, according to many leaders. Women are allowed to squeeze into the liturgy only after lay men have paved the way. Right now the same strategy is being used for the diaconate: "Let's see how our male deacons are accepted and then if it all gets worked out we can let women in too." But to anyone who believes that women are innately psychologically different from men (and this includes most of the clergy) or those who believe women bring different experiences (this includes almost everybody) it should be obvious that women have to be involved in forming new liturgical roles, not just shoved into the molds that men have made in their own image.

Why then do women remain reluctant to break the barrier? Many denominations report that their women are more adamant in holding the old sex barriers in the churches than men are. And letters to editors on the popular level often show an attitude that women should not be up in front reading or performing in church because their job is to make a good Christian home, as though the pew were any closer to home than the lectern.

The use of women in the liturgy is clearly highly symbolic and charged with meaning for many people. And many women find it threatening, an indication that women have a task far beyond bearing and raising children and keeping house. The more traditional churches especially find that the words "Women's Liberation" automatically flash "ungodly" to many of their members, and women in any sort of officiating capacity in the liturgy represent a personal affront. There are deep psychological fears involved.

An understanding and kindly woman who has spent decades working with Protestant women's groups put it thoughtfully, "We have to be very careful in talking about women's responsibility today to our women who have devoted their lives to taking care of their families and doing volunteer work for the church, because it raises the problem for them that perhaps they didn't choose wisely."

Problems like this arise often for groups that act, or tell their people to act, upon moral or ethical judgments. One of the objections to withdrawal from Vietnam was that we couldn't admit that all those American boys had died in vain. Father Hans Küng makes clear that one of the big—or perhaps the biggest—objections to changing the Church's position on contraception was that tradition had already been established and many Catholics had made tremendous sacrifices. The Catholic Church faces this problem periodically: it's one of the reasons we are strong on the idea of "development of doctrine." It's typical of the whole set of tensions behind a good many of the credibility gaps in this world. Somewhere and sometime a practical judgment based on available experience has been presented as an eternal truth in order to "save the simple people from confusion." Catholicism was at one time opposed to lending money for interest, too. Over the years economic situations and social and secular structures change, and we find it difficult to change our ethical judgments of the prudent and sensible way to interpret the signs of the times.

This is the case with our attitude toward women and even sex in general. Not too long ago there was Christian opposition to pain-relievers in childbirth because of the statement in Genesis, "I shall multiply your pains in childbearing, you shall give birth to your children in pain." Up until almost the present some people were concerned if women appeared in Church without a head covering. Today it is often the sight of a woman in a public liturgical role which raises too many questions for some minds. It will take the combined efforts of priests and people to make the move to a liturgy consonant with today's sociological and theological understandings of woman as smooth as possible.

Men tend to underestimate their own role in giving women freedom to develop, In almost all cases women have been brought up to depend more upon the approval of the opposite sex than have men; the fact that women are more likely to be judged on their appearance and personality than on their attainments or job performance leaves them much more vulnerable to personal criticism—or compliments!

That means women need men in supportive roles, to encourage them, give them advice and help, and pitch in with the work. Women are constantly doing the same for men—busying themselves with most of the dirty work of typing and envelope stuffing in political campaigns, taking care of the details so that the businessman or scholar can get on with his project. Now it's time for paying back a little of the debt.

Our ecumenical group working on problems of women in organized religion in Philadelphia has specialized in putting on dozens of ecumenical panels on college campuses, in churches and synagogues, and at club meetings. Whenever possible the group likes to include a man on the panel, partly to show that many men are just as concerned as women about sexual injustice, that this mustn't be a war between the sexes, and also to prove that this isn't a "woman's problem," but a human problem. What we are concerned with ultimately is not feminine development but human development.

Liturgy might be a good place to begin some male-female cooperation. It's hard to think of an area in which women are more in need of a helping hand. And a good liturgy can't be one-half male and one-half female; it has to be the result of the two halves working and creating together.

Although things like reading the Scriptures at Mass or helping to distribute Communion have nothing to do with ordination to the priesthood or even the diaconate, they are important because the opponents of women in the priesthood are talking less and less about theological objections and more about sociological or psychological considerations. And here the objections to women in any sort of office are similar: it is contrary to custom and the people do not wish it. Both sides are quite aware that a woman in the pulpit has her foot in the clerical door.

One of the best ways to learn how we ourselves react to women at the altar or in the pulpit is to test ourselves. There are quite a few Protestant groups which ordain women, and a visit to a church where a woman is officiating is usually fairly simple to manage.

One Catholic woman invited a few years back to be part of an ecumenical retreat team for a Protestant group was extremely impressed to discover that the lay president of the women's group also presided at the Eucharist, although there were several ordained women present. Having the natural, elected leader of the organization also distributing the Eucharist seemed so right and logical that it was only in talking about it later that the Catholic woman stopped to think that this was the first time she had seen a woman at the altar. Sex didn't seem significant at all.

Women preachers come in all styles and levels, just as women teachers or men preachers do. Too often they don't have as much experience as their male counterparts, but they have just as much to say. One ordained Protestant woman who recently got a position teaching homiletics (preaching) in her denomination's seminary found that many of her friends were amazed—"I just can't imagine their letting a woman teach homiletics!" But why not, she asked? It's women who have had to sit in the pew and listen to all those sermons over the years!

In the past there have been a good many reasons given as to why women could not be priests in the Catholic Church. Some were scriptural, but none of the passages in the New Testament is really relevant to the question of ordination. Some arguments were rather peripheral at best, like the fact that Mary was not a priest. Some dealt with the order of creation, but Paul's statement that in Christ there is neither male nor female makes a pretty strong refutation. Perhaps the most usual argument on the popular level today is that Jesus did not choose women for Apostles. Of course he did not choose Gentiles either, so the argument is not convincing. There is rather general agreement that Jesus chose twelve Jewish males to represent the twelve tribes of the New Israel.

Theologians are still arguing the question, and church historians are still researching the past, but the consensus is now that there are no theological impediments to women priests. That leaves the question of tradition—or history—and the problem of general acceptance.

Recently the number of women seeking ordination in the Catholic Church or at least asking for a change in the legislation which forbids women priests has increased at a fast rate. During the Second Vatican Council the question was first raised publicly, and St. Joan's International Alliance began its annual petition for consideration of women priests. One of St. Joan's members, Mary B. Lynch, later became the first woman accepted as a student in a Catholic seminary.

Protestant groups are studying the question too. Those who do ordain women are now being accused of injustice in giving the women only those posts men do not want, such as working with children or supplying the tiny rural parishes. Those who did not ordain women are reconsidering their positions: most of the Lutheran groups in this country are now ordaining women, and even the Episcopal Church has moved in that direction. In the Catholic Church there have been recommendations for opening the diaconate to women. Only the Eastern Orthodox Churches remain completely closed to the question.

If women had full access to the decision making levels in the Church, what kind of changes could we expect? Well, there would be a few changes of a negative kind—eliminating some of the misogynist phraseology, like the "defiled like a menstruous woman" section of the Easter vigil. And there'd be somewhat less of the "Pray, brothers" approach and more of the "Pray, brothers and sisters." We wouldn't all be 11 sons of God," nor would the Beatitudes come out as "Happy the man."

We could expect some positive additions as well. The wedding rite might be the first to be rewritten, for it is incredible that only celibates can decide what married people will vow. There is a good deal of freedom allowed in putting the ceremony together now, but the rules are still made by priests.

The baptismal rite might be improved if married women were given some voice in the matter. Why must it be a cleric who performs the baptism? Why isn't the opportunity used to educate the parents on their rights and duties toward the child? The old churching ceremony, which reminded too many women of the rite of purification, has been done away with, but nothing has been substituted. (Baptism is itself an improvement over circumcision, of course, which is automatically limited to males.)

The big questions bothering us now in the liturgy are social ones. How do we make people feel part of a worshiping group? How do we express this unity to one another and in our communal prayer? How do we make people feel at home? How do we combine people of various backgrounds and ages in one celebration? In our society it is women who do the social tasks of making people welcome, introducing them to one another, making members of the group comfortable and worrying about fitting the odd ones in.

It's also women for the most part who have discovered how to communicate truths to children and women who take the time to work with tots. Women have a lot of what our liturgy needs.

The other basic ingredient we are seeking today is new ways, contemporary forms and styles, for expressing our relationship to God, our neighbor, and the universe. As these forms must also be expressive of the feminine experience and the feminine search, it is important that women be able to contribute their insights and talents.

There's a saying that the only things women can do better than men are bearing children and singing soprano, but Catholics have been pointing out that the Church disputes even this; some of our people still feel that any self-respecting cathedral choir should use little boys rather than female sopranos. In the less traditional church music, however, women have been using their creative talents along with the men; some of the most popular contemporary church music is written by women, like Sister Miriam Therese of the Medical Mission Sisters.

In the areas of posters and banners women artists are even more prominent. On the other hand, the only art form which still frightens most church people is also the only one dominated by women—the dance.

Not too many years ago quite a few Catholics were questioning whether we weren't putting far too much emphasis on the liturgy. Today we see it as the real unifying factor of the Catholic community, but the task of unifying the male and female halves—and expressing that unity—is still mostly before us.

Dr. Lois Gunden Clemens, a Mennonite woman who has served her church for many years, believes strongly in the differences between men and women. These very differences, she says, make it necessary to give women an equal voice in the church.

"From many directions authorities in various fields are suggesting that in the present state of affairs when the world is suffering from too much male assertiveness, what is needed above all else is a realization of the importance of interdependence and social cohesion in all human affairs. This calls for understanding in human relations, social poise, and the skill of persuasion, which are precisely the skills too often lacking in men's relationships with others. The women, for whom these interests and skills come naturally, should be having a more important role at all levels in the formulating of policy.

Woman, who stands for the significance of individual life, will be searching for what gives meaning and significance to life. While men establish laws and create philosophical systems, women will question their validity and challenge their authority. She is the one in the human partnership who could change into a home for humanity the society which has become depersonalized by man's techniques.

It must be recognized that from God's point of view it is much more important to be concerned about what is happening in the lives of human beings than to be concentrating on man's great achievements in the physical world. In the church there lurks the same danger. The excitement and satisfaction of achievement in programs and structured activity can be diverting attention from the real mission of the church to change lives. It is the quality of life and its expression in meaningful relationships the love one for another—that should be the distinguishing marks of the Christian community. If it is woman's natural concern to make possible a more abundant life, then she should be expressing her views in ways that count in the church." (Woman Liberated, Herald Press, 1971, pp. 82-83.)

> *What traits and talents do women especially have, either by their nature or through their experiences?*

How does the Church manifest itself as a male-dominated community?

In what ways do women have a specific contribution to make?

A noted Catholic theologian writes about the different ways in which women may react to the public image of woman today.

"Many women seem to collapse psychically under the sheer weight of the stereotypes dumped upon them. They lose their nerve and cannot believe in the truth of their own experience as persons. They settle for a pre-fabricated destiny and proceed to try to fulfill the stereotype, in the vain hope of gaining acceptance and approval. So they set out to be manageable accessories—shapeless, brainless, helpless, but efficient instruments for someone else's purpose. Anyone who resorts to this type of role-playing has to suppress frightening amounts of conflict and hostility, because she is utterly alienated from her true self and cannot afford to admit it. She may find free women a direct and intolerable threat to herself. She may need to be catty and underhanded to try to pull them down and destroy them." (Monika Hellwig, "Hope and Liberation," *Liturgy*, Oct. 1970, p. 14.)

How do women today experience themselves as persons?

Can they experience themselves as persons in the traditional role in the liturgy?

Why do some women prefer to retain and limit themselves to this traditional passive role?

Why do some women feel threatened by other women going beyond the traditional role?

Rev. Elsie Gibson of the United Church of Christ has written a book about women ministers based on interviews and questionnaires sent to several hundred ordained women.

"Opinions as to whether or not ordination is a right for which women should contend differ among female clergy themselves. Marie Hubbel, who has been a pastor in California and is now doing graduate work, tells ordained women, 'Never, for whatever provocation, take up the cause of women's rights. For us to espouse this cause is to lose friends and influence.'...

Militancy on the part of a woman minister places men on the defensive. Their reaction may be a combination of semi-guilt over an unfair situation they feel personally powerless to remedy and irritation with the woman for making a fuss about what cannot be helped. The issue is similar to that of civil rights; there is an additional difficulty in that relationships between men and women are even more complicated and delicate than those between races.

It seems to me that men can do more for women in this regard than women can do for themselves. If, for example, a man believes he has received a real call to

ministry, how can he face God in prayer and deny a woman the privilege of responding to the same invitation? I believe that the great majority of Christian men will defend women in their desire to serve God, once they grasp the spiritual import of what is being asked." (*When the Minister is a Woman*, Holt, Rinehart and Winston, 1970, pp. 70-71.)

> *A good many ordained women, especially younger ministers, have reacted negatively to passages like this. Do you think their irritation is justified?*

> *How can Catholic men—lay and priests—help women? Will they do so?*

> *How can women enlist their aid?*

5. BEYOND THE COLLECTION BASKET

Women thinking about their position in the Catholic Church often have to stop to ask whether they are being accurate. Is it women who have no authority over the expenses and budgeting of the parish, or is it laypeople in general? Is it women who are under-represented in the liturgical commissions and committees of the dioceses and parishes or is it just lay women who are overlooked? (Sisters are, of course, technically laypeople also, but their position and role in the Church are so different from other women's that they are popularly thought of as a separate category.)

People are becoming increasingly aware that the Catholic Church is excessively clerical. All the functions of the organization—executive, judicial, and legislative, as well as the allotment of monies and official theorizing—are done almost exclusively by priests and bishops. The entire Church, clergy and laity, has gone along with this system for so long that it's ingrained in all of us, and there's no sense in pointing fingers. There are people on both sides trying to overcome the division: priests are looking for lay people to form part of the parochial team and share decision-making and work, and lay people are searching for responsibility in their parishes. Unfortunately there aren't nearly enough of either.

But even this would be a mere first step at a time when women are demanding to go all the way—and fast. Why, they ask, should not qualified women run the diocesan social service offices and allocate funds, when it is clearly women and children who are most in need? Why shouldn't qualified women—especially married women—run the Family Life offices and act as judges in the ecclesiastical marriage courts? Why shouldn't women have equal voice in managing and staffing the seminaries training servants for the entire People of God? The questions get louder and louder.

Women have not been very successful in getting professional positions high up on the policy-making levels in any of the Christian churches. Several of the major Protestant denominations have made surveys of women's employment in the past few years, and in no case were the women happy about the results of their surveys.

An interesting example is a study of employment on the national level by the American Baptist Convention. The ABC, in a tradition of sexual equality, has been ordaining women for more than eighty years, and it has had several women presidents of the Church.

Rev. Elizabeth Miller found in this study that the merger of the men's and women's Mission Societies in 1948 meant that the number of executive positions held by women has lessened. The women's groups had also served as a sort of training ground for church executives, and their loss and the fact that there are now only 4 women to 78 men at the department head level (the first rank above the basic professional level) means there is little hope that women can be promoted to the higher levels. (In 1958 the ABC had ten women department heads or equivalents.) The author points out that on the national and also the local levels, reorganization often means that the women are "reorganized out."

Why the change? The Rev. Ms. Miller suggests several reasons: the attitude of society that men are the supervisors and women are the supervised, and the unwritten assumption that pastoral experience is necessary for most executive positions while at the same time women are discouraged from pastoral work. But she also states, "in some instances the replacement of women by men in staff positions was done deliberately in order to increase the status of the job or to 'change the image' of the work from being an interest of women to a work of interest that should involve men. Little thought, however, was given to what this concern, about 'status' or 'image' said to women about themselves or to the Convention about its attitude toward women."

Employment in the Catholic Church is still more difficult for women, because our structure is still more clerical. Unlike the Baptists, it is not necessarily pastoral experience but only the reception of Holy Orders which is a prerequisite for almost any job of importance. There are a lot of employment possibilities in peripheral areas, but the big offices where policy is made are almost entirely clerical, and the few laypeople hired on the administrative level are usually all men.

Thus the diocesan chief superintendent of schools is almost always a priest and—up until 1972—was always a man. The heads of Family Life Bureaus are priests. Yet most of the teachers in the system are female, as are half of the married people.

Women are making inroads in some of these areas. In 1968 Pittsburgh became the first U.S. diocese to prepare civil lawyers to work in ecclesiastical marriage courts. They get a special course in canon law and papers and cases to study. These lay lawyers are a great success; the petitioners identify much more easily with lay advocates.

Such situations are still unusual. The average woman seeking an annulment from the church has priests as defender, prosecutor, and judge. She will not even be free to take a woman lawyer with her to the trial. Unless she is very unusual, the whole business will be unnecessarily humiliating and threatening.

Another reason women are not succeeding in finding good professional positions is the lack of real recruitment procedures. High executive staff positions are never advertised, and in one recent case a priest who did place a notice in a newspaper was called on the carpet by his bishop. The important policy-making positions in any diocese will ordinarily be filled by the patronage system: the bishop appoints the men he wants.

The situation in church structures outside the regular diocesan system is just as frustrating. There are, for example, lots of good competent women theologians looking for college teaching jobs. A few years ago all looked well for their employment, and the Placement Bureau of the College Theology Society reported that very few schools scouting for new instructors specified either sex. But now positions are fewer. Not only is the competition keener, but women don't even get into the competition. Half a dozen Catholic colleges surveyed informally this year all indicate that they are hiring new faculty in an unorganized way. They do not go to college placement bureaus; they do not place ads; they don't even ask for recommendations from local graduate schools.

This is typical of all departments in today's colleges and universities. When there is a position open, the present faculties are consulted for suggestions, and males tend to have male friends they want to help. This "grapevine system" means that few women even get to hear about openings. Even men who are unemployed contend it's a pretty undemocratic and inefficient way to operate.

Jobs are opening up in other areas, especially those where the team concept is developing. College campuses, for example, are now likely to talk about a team chaplaincy, a term that emphasizes the advantages of having different kinds of people with differing backgrounds and experiences working together. Sometimes the formation of the team itself shows a different kind of prejudice, with the emphasis on getting a nun—a more official type of female—rather than a woman with relevant experiences like college teaching or marriage and family. As a matter of fact, though many women—Sisters and lay women—are working to break down the artificial male-female barriers, too often they are not even aware of their own Sisters vs. laywomen prejudices. Real church teamwork is still a long way off.

The Sisters who are working in campus ministry are both successful and enthusiastic. Often they start with the assumption that they will be counseling the young women and are surprised to find themselves spending more time talking with the male students. Besides counseling they do almost everything the priest chaplain does: arrange ecumenical activities, plan liturgies, teach, organize courses.

One Protestant woman minister says she's enthusiastic about her work as campus minister but even more enthusiastic about the fact that she and her husband form a team. Working together, they bring two viewpoints to every subject, their opinions on sexual questions are taken much more seriously, their home has become a real center for religious discussion and activity.

In fields like retreat work women can make a real contribution. Who but a Sister can understand the problems of religious women? Who but a married woman can put the doubts and problems of today's wives and mothers into words and suggest solutions? The days are past when we thought that all people faced the same temptations and needed the same advice, but we are only beginning to see that the knowledge necessary for guiding people comes not from books but from having struggled with the problems for ourselves.

Journalism has always been an area in which women were comparatively easily accepted, and for the most part this is true in religious journalism, though there are still editors who think that religious news means news about priests and that only men reporters can work with priests. Today's religious educators and parish coordinators are often women too.

The other positions with power in the churches—or in any organization—are the board memberships. This is where more general policy questions are decided and where, often, funds are allocated and statements written and released. These positions are not held by paid employees but by "volunteers." There is always a distinct difference between, board and staff of any organization.

In the Catholic Church in this country there are two boards, the United States Catholic Conference and the National Conference of Catholic Bishops. They are really the same group—the US bishops—operating under two different names when they deal with internal and external problems. Not only is it impossible for a woman to be a member of either of these boards, but it is virtually impossible for her to appear to testify at any of their meetings.

The various Protestant churches deal with this question in different ways. The Episcopalians, for example, in their triennial meetings, have two houses, and women can be elected delegates to the lower house. Presbyterians have strong lay rule; each presbytery (comparable to a diocese) has both clerical and lay delegates from each member church, and women are eligible in both categories, though of course they are never represented in anything like their real proportion of the membership.

The women of the Christian Church (Disciples of Christ) recently decided it was necessary to tell people the facts about their church, one of the more liberal on the woman question. Their Department of Christian Women's Fellowship recently issued a flyer headed with a big sign, "We have listened . . Now we want to Join the ACTION!" and signed "Women of the Christian Church." They started out with some "Facts and Fallacies" like these.

> FALLACY: Since women have the equal opportunity with men to be elected to any office of the church, women have served in all positions.

FACT: No woman has ever been elected moderator of the General Assembly or president of the International Convention.

FALLACY: Women have been elected to top positions on the general staffs of the Christian Church.

FACT: No woman has ever been the top executive of a board or agency of the church, and few women are in advanced staff positions.

The flyer quotes two pages of statistics to show that although women make up 32% of the General Board, the committees appointed or approved by the General Board contain only 19% women. And the boards of the Units—or agencies of the Christian Church are only 10% women.

It becomes clear that just making a change in rules—allowing women to be ordained or ecclesiastical professionals will not of itself insure a real change in women's status and role unless it is accompanied by a real education of all the members, male and female, cleric and lay. At the same time it is clearer than ever that reeducation of attitudes will do nothing without a simultaneous change in laws.

Historians of the woman suffrage movement in America have been wondering why feminism more or less collapsed several decades ago. The reason seems to be that feminists set their hearts on the vote and in their working toward that goal convinced themselves it was the answer to all women's problems. It wasn't, of course, because women have to be trained to use their power of suffrage intelligently. But at least women now have the tool to free themselves. Church laws can be changed, too, to give women opportunity to see what sorts of contributions they might make.

Still the Church is much more than a group of people who devote themselves to its work for their livelihood or who get together in small groups to decide what the rest of us are going to do. Not many women—or men—can operate on those levels, or would even want to. The important thing is that the best available talent be used for God's work in the Church and that the needs, the insights and the experiences of all the People of God be gathered together in the Church's thinking.

These ordinary laypeople need from their Church a chance to contribute something to the total Catholic community beyond the Sunday collections. Too often no opportunity is available. And, just because Father finds it more convenient and comfortable to confer with men, it's usually the case that the women are even more limited than the men. This is especially unfortunate, because Catholic women are still often told to stay at home and mind the house rather than the store, and they more than their husbands need ways in which to make a meaningful contribution to society.

If parish councils—the elected, not the appointed kind—get a real start, and women are encouraged to run for parish offices, the whole process of change may begin there. But again, only a small fraction of parish members can be on the council at one time.

One of the big tasks of any Christian community should be to create groups and channels through which members can give of themselves in order to help others. Task forces, work-days, ad hoc committees all should be available. Instead we often find card parties and dances to raise money for somebody else to go out and do something Christian.

If women educate the children in school and at home, why don't they figure more prominently on school boards? Why aren't former nurses trained as volunteer hospital visitors for the parish? Why aren't the women of the parish asked to make parish surveys to discover the problems of the needy, who will for the most part be women and children?

Ecumenism is a good example. At the moment we don't need a lot more theologizing—the structures are already far behind in finding ways to implement the findings. What we need is a large amount of grass-roots getting to know each other, visiting back and forth, experiencing one another's forms of worship, planning for the ecumenical future. And women would have a lot to offer in this kind of situation. Just by training and experience, they know how to plan a pleasant social evening, how to help people meet other Christians as people, how to keep a conversation going. Yet ecumenism is hardly ever a lay affair. No wonder people find it boring!

Whenever any group is considered inferior and relegated to the drudge jobs, its members tend to lose ambition. After a few genera-tions they may be convinced they never had any ambition, that to be content with a job in which one cannot exercise one's mind is simply natural. Most Sisters don't think it strange that although they cannot enter a seminary as students or teach in it, they are expected to do the cooking and cleaning.

With expectations, ambitions—andwill—blunted, the first move of any newly-conscious oppressed group is usually an attempt at self-consciousness and self-determination. The group decides to run its own schools and own affairs, and "colonialists," or members of the oppressor group, are not very welcome except in a strictly supportive capacity, and sometimes not even then.

The strange thing is that the Catholic Church is the one institution which has women's "separatist" organizations built right into its traditions, and they are as yet unused. The religious orders still have female inferiority written into them, with the Sisters being subject to male clerics in the parish, diocesan, and world levels.

But the women's schools are a different matter. Separate education for women in Catholicism has a different purpose than in the secular world, where the great women's colleges were formed to give wom-en an opportunity for education in a day when all the existing colleges and universities were limited to males. In the Catholic Church women's schools were started as a method of keeping wom-en separate and teaching them to be women, i.e., docile wives. It also gave Sisters an opportunity to teach, because it was often considered unseemly for them to be teaching males.

Still Sisters have more of a tradition of development of oneself and one's talents than most laywomen do, and there is a lot of talk about self-discovery in recruiting women for women's schools and colleges. There is a lot to be hoped for.

At this point it is still mostly hope. In many ways Catholic schools are moving backwards, as people like Father Andrew Greeley have been noting for several years now.

Situations in other church groups are not necessarily better. The United Presbyterian Church in the USA, for example, recently made a study of its 46 church-related colleges and came up with some dismal statistics. None of the 46, it discovered, had a woman as chairman of the Board of Trustees (or Directors), and 'there are very few women on the boards at all. Ten colleges have no women trustees. Two colleges, Wilson and Beaver, have 36% and 33% women trustees, but that's not very impressive when we realize they are women's colleges! And none of these 46 institutions has a woman president.

If schools and colleges are really to be run in a way to allow women to discover themselves without spending their energies impressing males, to determine their own likes and ambitions, and to become seriously involved in helping to determine the future, there are a number of things which would have to be provided:

1. A large proportion (perhaps three-fourths) of the faculty would have to be women. These women would have to be seriously dedicated to teaching and to scholarship. The fact that they would not be inferior in competence to the men on the faculty would be reflected in the fact that women would hold a proportionate (three-fourths) number of department chairmanships etc.

2. The faculty would provide good examples, or role models, of women following various patterns. There should be dedicated Sisters, but also happy dedicated single professional women and at least as many women who are successfully combining scholarship and family life. Teachers with young children might need some special schedule juggling for a few years, but their example would be more than worth the trouble.

3. The school would help to destroy the myth that women can't get along together and prefer men for bosses by keeping women in the top administrative positions—certainly the presidency, and at least three fourths of the other positions as well as the board of trustees.

4. Although women's colleges traditionally focus on the liberal arts, they would need a strong program of vocational guidance.

5. Women students need the opportunity of seeing and talking with successful women in various fields and professions. At least three-fourths of the commencement speakers, award winners,

43

and outside lecturers on campus or in assemblies would be women.

Most Catholic women's colleges and schools would flunk this test. It's quite clear that women today can't blame men for all their problems.

Prof. Rosemary Ruether of Howard University sees several special tasks for women's colleges:

"Women's colleges are natural sources of institutional power for women in society, and they should be used more consciously as such (just as Negroes are discovering that the Negro college, also founded under conditions of discrimination, is a source of black institutional power in society)...

Both women and the women's college have a special freedom to demythologize the work culture which dominates current education, and to keep the cultivation of the whole man in view as the real horizon both of education and of life." ("Are Women's Colleges Obsolete?" *The Critic*, Oct.-Nov. 1968, p. 64.)

In what ways could women's colleges fulfill the two tasks suggested by Dr. Ruether?

To what extent do the Catholic women's colleges and schools in your experience recognize the tasks? implement them?

The Catholic Citizen, the Journal of St. Joan's Alliance, recently reported:

"Bishop Gran of Oslo speaking for the Scandinavian Bishops' Conference on the question of priestly celibacy favored the acceptance of some married priests. He referred to the marriages of Lutheran clergy, whose wives play an important part in parish affairs. He added 'They are good housekeepers, something not to be overlooked at a time when servants have become practically extinct and the number of nuns is diminishing.' " (Nov.-Dec. 1971, p. 143.)

What are the advantages for women of a celibate clergy?

What are the disadvantages?

To what extent are nuns seen as the servants of priests?

Make your own survey. Identify the positions of power in your diocese. You might want to use three categories: those which need specific theological training (dogma professor at seminary); those which need specific training in other fields (editor of diocesan newspaper); those which merely require ability and willingness to dig in and work (members of diocesan ecumenical commission).

Do any in the first category actually require ordination—do they require the saying of Mass or hearing of confessions?

How many of these positions are held by priests? Sisters? lay men? lay women?

6. WHAT'S A GOOD MARRIAGE AND WHO DECIDES?

If men have decided what they wanted women to be, it's even more obvious that they have a stake in what marriage is. In the past few decades, especially as women got the vote and later went into politics, marriage has been in theory a union of two equals. Marriage was what the two individuals made it.

But this has been less true in the Catholic church. All the laws, theology, rights and rites are still determined by men, and for the most part by unmarried men at that. Take the *New Catholic Encyclopedia*, published in 1967 (the last *Catholic Encyclopedia* was published in 1913, so we can expect this one to be with us a long time!). In this 1967 version, there are 20 signed articles on marriage, one on marriage counseling, four on abortion, one on contraception, one on engagement, four on divorce, one on sex, one on sex education, and one on sex in the Bible, one on courtship, and one on dating; these are all signed articles with only a few of the authors writing more than one of these 35 articles. And every one is written by a male. Most are by priests.

But while theologizing and legislating on marriage seems to be thought of as man's work, current church thinking seems to indicate that the job of making the marriage work belongs to the woman. A man may be a salesman, doctor or teacher —and oh, yes, he's married too; but a woman is primarily married, and then maybe a typist or nurse when there's time.

This means a woman is pressured to plan for either marriage or a serious career, and not both together. The two options are made to seem opposed to one another. The desire for achievement, and this includes even intellectual achievement, is labeled aggressive, unfeminine. Dr. Matina Horner, who has studied the problem, writes, "Consciously or unconsciously the girl equates intellectual achievement with loss of femininity. A bright woman is caught in a double bind. In testing and other achievement-oriented situations she worries not only about failure, but also about success. If she fails, she is not living up to her own standards of performance; if she succeeds she is not living up to societal expectations about the female role. Men in our society do not experience this kind of ambivalence, because they are not only permitted but actively encouraged to do well."

Dr. Horner's technique to discover "motive to avoid success" was to give tests to a sample of 90 girls and 88 boys at the University of Michigan. As part of the test each was asked to write a continuation to a story: "After first-term finals, John (Anne) finds himself (herself) at the top of his (her) medical-school class." The girls wrote about Anne and the boys about John.

Fewer than ten percent of the men showed evidence of the motive to avoid success, but over sixty-five percent of the women did. Some typical responses:

> She studies 12 hours a day, and lives at home to save money. "Well it certainly paid off. All the Friday and Saturday nights without dates, fun—I'll be the best woman doctor alive." And yet a twinge of sadness comes through—she wonders what she really has....

> Anne feels guilty.... She will finally have a nervous breakdown and quit medical school and marry a successful young doctor.

> Anne is talking to her counselor. Counselor says she will make a fine nurse.

The male responses were far different:

> John has worked very hard and his long hours of study have paid off.... He is thinking about his girl, Cheri, whom he will marry at the end of med. school. He realizes he can give her all the things she desires after he becomes established. He will go on in med. school and be successful in the long run.

Sensitive parents have been aware of the problem for years. More and more they worry about the anti-intellectual and anti-achievement pressures their daughters suffer from television, magazines, and even in their schools and churches. Some parents go out of their way to find women doctors for the family; some make it a point to take children to concerts with women soloists or lectures by women specialists.

A survey of some prominent Catholic married women made in 1971 revealed they felt they had to fight the going image. One mother said, "Never let secretary, nurse, or assistant role be talked of without encouraging her to be doctor, boss, scientist-president." And this woman added that she has special difficulties because her six-year-old daughter already tends to see herself as subordinate to her boss/brothers. Another said that "the sky's the limit" in encouraging vocational ideals for daughters.

Remaining to be tackled—and tackled vigorously—is the problem of the narrow stereotyping our society and educational systems impose on boys. Women have been complaining about being locked out of certain vocational areas. A few men are beginning to ask whether it's any better to be locked in.

Marriage today is being seen more and more as a partnership, a sort of democratic commitment between two people. Today there is no more doubt about the equality of the sexes—it has been demonstrated that women are as intelligent as men, stay on their jobs as long as men do, have physical endurance equal to a man's. A family is a team, making decisions communally. A lot of this new attitude comes as a result of women's civic equality. If a woman's vote counts as much as a man's vote in a civic election, why should she suddenly be less important than he in making a family decision which will affect her even more immediately?

'Way back in the last century when the whole question of women's suffrage came up, there were many people who sensed that giving the vote to women meant the opening of the door to a lot of other possibilities. Today their fears are amusing. Orestes Brownson, the great American Catholic philosopher of the nineteenth century, predicted that husbands and wives would run against each other for office, women would run off to Congress or the battlefield instead of taking care of their children, abortion would increase "and the human race be threatened with extinction"—all as a result of giving women the vote.

Today in many places in this country women are still not treated equally by the law: they are forbidden to keep their own names, they are granted alimony, they may not go into business without their husband's consent, they are more easily released from jury duty. But with even one woman in the US Senate and a handful in the House of Representatives women know that in theory they are equal collaborators in the government and are refusing to accept a lesser role in their marriages.

But laws are changed more easily than attitudes. And our traditions go back into dim history, where women have always been valued mostly as wives—as child-bearing animals—both in the classic Greco-Roman tradition and in the ancient Hebrew tradition. It was Demosthenes who said, "We have courtesans for pleasure, slave women for personal service and wives to bear us lawful offspring and be faithful guardians of our houses."

The ancient Hebrews considered women just another form of property, as did their contemporaries—and as do some of ours! A man's house included his family, servants, animals and home, all of which belonged to him. The same concept can be found still in Paul's writings (and other epistles) where slaves, children, and wives are told to be obedient to the pater familias.

This was the reason that adultery was considered so much more serious on the part of a woman. The husband's property was being used by another man. A man's unfaithfulness was considerably less serious; some people think it still is.

> The patriarchal system of today's family shows up very clearly in the horror with which many people hear of the suggestion that a woman should not give up her name when she marries.
>
> A man's wife, like his slaves in an earlier day, is expected to be identified as his. More and more women are rebelling at such a system, not because they love their husbands any less, but because they feel they too are people with their own identities. Can you imagine, they ask, a man wanting to be known by his wife's name? A woman today expects to grow and mature all her life, not to settle into a rigid role, and she wants to continue being herself for all these years.

There are levels to the name question. If a woman does give up her own family name at marriage and take that of her husband, why should she also use his first name? Why shouldn't she at least be Mrs. Mary Smith? In their own way, first names are perhaps even more important than family names. They are highly symbolic. In primitive cultures, to know a person's name was to have power over him remember the story of Rumpelstiltskin? In religion a first name is extremely important. It is given in the sacrament of baptism; the name ordinarily is that of a saint with whom the child will identify and whom he or she will imitate.

Formerly sisters and priests in religious orders were given new names when they took their vows, as a symbol of a break with the past and the beginning of a new identity. The popes and some monarchs—still take on a new name as they assume office and become more an official than a person.

Some women are beginning to re-think their habits. Recently the Chicago Archdiocesan Council of Catholic Women voted in convention that "Whereas, The need for communication among women for a more personal recognition is recognized; Resolved, That the Archdiocesan Council of Catholic Women compile all roster sheets with the woman's first name and her husband's first name in parenthesis. Example: Mary Smith (Mrs. John L.)"

Another level is the very use of the word Miss or Mrs. at all. The solution now being proposed is the word Ms., pronounced Miz. It's an answer that makes a lot of people unhappy. One Catholic college chaplain protested, "But you're taking women's identity away." It is true that to almost everyone it's more important to be able to pinpoint a woman's marital status than it is to know a man's personal life. And unfortunately we do judge a woman to a great extent by her relations to men. The pressures on a woman to marry are strong.

When she does marry, she is most likely given the status of her husband. Perhaps this is why the higher the social class the more likely the woman is to use her husband's first name on public occasions. Without his achievement she is nothing. When a woman on an important board was asked recently why all the women were listed by their husband's first and last names, she said with a smile, "They prefer it that way. They know they wouldn't be there except for their husbands."

The status of First Lady we give the wife of the president of the country or a smaller political unit or even a corporation or university is another example of the way our society rewards non-achievement in women. Any First Lady is expected to *be* charming, beautiful and well dressed, but she's not expected to *do* much. And none of these qualities is demanded of her. At the same time the woman who is a senator, a State official, a brilliant scientist or scholar will have far less status in the public eye: little girls will not hang her picture on their walls alongside their more glamourous role-models.

Among the upper classes, as well as those who like to think of themselves as upper class (and that includes quite a few people), a non-working wife is a status symbol. Certain groups seem to exert special pressures on their members to keep their wives out of paying jobs—doctors, armed forces officers, and ministers are typical. To some extent these wives are kept busy in their husband's work, whether attending medical auxiliary functions, being very busy in local projects in a very visible way as service wives, or doing all sorts of unpaid sub-professional jobs in the local parish.

Betty Friedan quoted in 1963 from a "Suggested Outline for Married Couples' Discussions" from the New York Archdiocese's Family Life Bureau. The panels of married couples, she says, were directed to raise the question "Can a working wife be a challenge to the authority of the husband?" The engaged couples who made up the audience were to have pointed out to them that the wife who works "may be subtly undermining her husband's sense of vocation as the breadwinner and head of the house. The competitive business world can inculcate in the working bride attitudes and habits which may make it difficult for her to adjust to her husband's leadership. . . ."

A book on "The Executive's Wife" states that, "Studies show that executives, more than any other group of husbands, do not want their wives to work. Unexpectedly, opposition is not primarily because of a challenge to their earning power, but because they 'prefer their wives to be free to take care of their creature comforts and to provide the proper home setting for their own careers.'"

Proper home setting, of course, includes not only creating a pleasant atmosphere, but entertaining in the proper manner. The same author writes, "Today, it is agreed, very few men reach the top brass classification unless their wives are socially acceptable."

All this makes it quite clear that among large segments of the educated and well-to-do, child-raising has nothing to do with a disapproval of working wives. In fact, it is no exaggeration to say that many of these professional wives are gone more than working wives, and that they are much more likely to be gone in the dinner hour and the evening when the children are at home.

On the other hand, devoting one's life to raising children has never been the usual task for women in the past. Sociologist Alice S. Rossi writes, ". . . For the first time in the history of any known society, motherhood has become a full time occupation for adult women. In the past, whether a woman lived on a farm, a Dutch city in the seventeenth century, or a colonial town in the eighteenth century, women in all strata of society except the very top were never able to be full-time mothers as the twentieth-century middle class American woman has become. These women were productive members of farm and craft teams along with their farmer, baker or printer husbands and other adult kin. Children either shared in the work of the household or were left to amuse themselves; their mothers did not have the time to organize their play, worry about their development, discuss their problems."

So how does this all affect young people either married or about to get married today? Long before they are thinking about getting married or even thinking about thinking about getting married the pressures are at work.

Marriage is expected to be a partnership, with each person making a unique contribution toward the common goal. Husbands and wives ought to be chosen for most of the same qualities we choose best friends and business partners for, and then something else besides. Society however expects us to choose our mates on qualities like prettiness and vivaciousness or athletic ability and money. Pressures differ from age group to age group and class to class, but almost anyone honest can think of someone of the opposite sex who would make a great friend and companion but is too tall or too short, too athletic or too bookish, too dark or too light, or just not good-looking enough. Even priests were heard to complain about Jacqueline

Kennedy's marriage to someone as old and apparently as unattractive as Mr. Onassis.

When two people do find themselves attracted to one another, the whole question of sexual morals comes to plague them. There seems to have been a double standard of sexual morality from the beginning of time, or at least since primitive man discovered that those babies had something to do with what he and his cave woman had been doing lying on the bearskins at night.

As it's always been the women who had the babies, it's always been easier to see whether the woman had been having sexual intercourse; and as the children have been the property of the husband, the need to know that the wife's children were also his has been important. The Old Testament treated adultery in women as much more serious than adultery in men. Women have protested this double standard. The women's convention in Seneca Falls in 1848, which was the beginning of the women's suffrage movement in this country, resolved that "the same amount of virtue, delicacy, and refinement of behavior that is required of woman in the social state should also be required of man, and the same transgressions should be visited with equal severity on both man and woman."

Catholics too often support the double standard by stressing that the woman is responsible for keeping the relationship on the proper level before marriage. All sorts of unfortunate attitudes follow from this. The woman has been so imbued with the idea that men are so sex-driven that they are really fairly irresponsible that she often confesses to feeling insulted if the man doesn't make some sort of attack at least the second or third time out. And the man can be made to feel that there's something peculiar about him if he does have himself under control. The whole idea of "machismo," strongly sexed masculine activity, thrives in many Catholic countries, as does the double standard.

When a couple marries, sexual adjustment is made more difficult if the male has been brought up to display and encourage his sexual drives and the woman has been trained to call the halt. And if the woman has become accustomed to holding the power of decision, and directing the man's impulses into all sorts of romantic channels, real live sex can come as a shock.

There are lots of other problems besides sexual adjustment after marriage, especially for a woman who wants to continue acting as a responsible self-directed adult.

Sociologists have studied family power systems, measuring power by who makes the family decisions on things like choosing the husband's job, the family car, and the house and deciding on vacations, life insurance and whether the wife will work. Recently Dair L. Gillespie has argued that our whole economic and social structure works against an equal voice for women in marriage.

The young couple may start out as more or less equal in the family decision-making process; they may even have talked it all over and decided that they will work together to keep things that way. But even the law is against them: the woman is obliged to take her husband's name, and she is legally bound to perform the housework and take care of her husband and children and he is legally obliged to support the family. If the wife works too, that's fine, but it's just an extra.

Whether the wife works or not, the husband's job will take a major role in determining the family life. If the wife works, she will automatically receive less money except in very rare cases, and with the husband the breadwinner, his job takes precedence. Sociologists have found that the higher the husband's occupational prestige, the higher his income, and the higher his status, the more power he has at home. Of course where to live, when to take a vacation, whom to be friends with, all depend largely on the man's job.

Later on, financially successful families tend to move to the suburbs. There, with the wife comparatively immobile, she will feel more and more isolated from what's going on in the world. She will lose contact with her old friends and depend more and more on her husband for knowledge of the world and for social life. She feels less and less like an equally intelligent adult.

As children come, she devotes her time to them and feels less and less capable of coping with problems in the world. Often she gets to the point where she dreads going to new places or traveling alone; she doesn't trust her judgments on politics or economics; she's afraid to tackle any community problems involving organizing and decision-making.

More and more women are growing unhappy over the situation. The more they are educated, and the more they read about all those time-saving devices, the more wrong it seems for them to be out of the mainstream of life. Other women, though happy raising their children, find themselves with nothing to do as they get older. The idea of returning to a job prepared for years before sounds much easier than it really is, and going back to school takes more courage and energy than most people—men or women—can pull together. How many men are willing to undergo job retraining?

The husband usually gets the blame for all this. But, although he is less likely to say so, he may be just as unhappy and confused about how all this happened to two such well-meaning people.

He, for example, though he does get out of the house each day to go to work, bears all the worry about making a living and getting a promotion. No wonder the life-expectancy statistics favor women! His wife, remembering that she had to give up her job and chance at some sort of professional status to assume his status, feels she has a right to rise to executive-wife or First Lady. She'll be helpful to him in climbing the ladder, but he knows that she is expecting him to be the man who gets the big promotion and so are the wives of nine other men. Nine of the ten will be disappointed, and nine men will be made to feel failures. When giving a wife the money to get the right kind of clothes and be active in the right kinds of activities is a sign of success, it does degrade the wife; but what happens to the man who doesn't make that sort of money?

Granted that it's difficult for a wife to have to move to a new neighborhood or a new part of the country to accommodate her husband's job, but often it's he who's left with the responsibility of supplying her with a social life in his spare time.

The feminine wife can become quite a burden.

Lots of people who say they are shocked by the idea of the working mother really are more concerned about "depriving the male of his primary breadwinning role" or "reducing the husband to co-housekeeper." Both of these are possibilities, and there are many people mostly women, of course—who think it might be a good idea if these things really came about.

Children themselves need not really suffer. In fact, specialists who have studied the facts point out that psychological problems and juvenile delinquency are no greater for children of working mothers than for other children.

There can be great advantages to working parents. The father can grow much closer to his children if he takes on his share of child-rearing, and some men are discovering that being a father is just as fulfilling as being a mother is for a woman. Any woman who has been both a working and a non-working mother knows that when she has fewer hours with her children she really spends those hours carefully— it's the quality, not the quantity, that matters. An intelligent educated woman with a job has her own plans and future to think about, and she is far less likely to become an overbearing mother directing her children's lives.

Just as the liberation of the Blacks means a liberation for the Whites, we cannot liberate one sex without the other. Sidney Cornelia Callahan, who is much concerned with what she calls "children's liberation," sums it up nicely: "With the proper safeguards for everyone's unique situation, we can create social solutions in which men, women, and children can be liberated together."

At the end of 1971 two lists of Most Admired Women appeared in the daily press. The first was a result of a poll by Good Housekeeping magazine, which sent a slate of 28 candidates to a sampling of one thousand members of its consumer panel. The second list comes from the Gallup Poll, in which 1504 persons, chosen to represent the entire adult population 18 years and over, were asked to list their choices without being given any suggestions.

GOOD HOUSEKEEPING

1. Mrs. Rose Kennedy

2. Mrs. Dwight D. Eisenhower

3. Miss Pearl S. Buck

4. Patricia Neal

5. Mrs. Richard M. Nixon

6. Golda Meir

7. Mrs. Ethel Kennedy

8. Helen Hayes

9. Indira Gandhi

10. Princess Grace of Monaco

GALLUP POLL

1. Golda Meir

2. Mrs. Richard M. Nixon

3. Mrs. Joseph P. Kennedy

4. Indira Gandhi

5. Mrs. Dwight D. Eisenhower

6. Mrs. Aristotle Onassis

7. Mrs. Lyndon B. Johnson

8. Mrs. John N. Mitchell

9. Senator Margaret Chase Smith

10. Rep. Shirley Chisholm

How many of these women are on the lists by virtue of their achievements? How many are included because of their marriages?

How many are engaged in "feminine" professions? How many could compete on a list of most admired people, both men and women?

What differences do you see in the two lists? How do you account for the variations?

Try making your own list.

A psychology professor tells about his experiences in Men's Liberation discussion groups:

> "A man must never admit to being hurt. That ruse starts with the young boy roughed up in a game who learns to shrug it off and say it's nothing. In later years, executives are conditioned out of humaneness: they are promoted for their ability to make the 'hard decisions'; which really means they've run roughshod over the human factors in a situation....

"One man mentioned how embarrassed he was when he checked into a big hotel one day, and since he was carrying both his own and his wife's luggage, she held the doors open for him. He worried about what the doorman, the reservation clerk and the other hotel guests might be thinking of him. Then he got furious with himself for even being bothered by the whole ridiculous thing. From that story we got into a whole thing about *why* he was carrying the bags in the first place ....

"Another fellow ... found himself really threatened when someone in his family suggested they didn't like their family name and wanted it changed. He suddenly realized that it was a traumatic thing for him to consider giving up his last name, and he said he'd never realized before that, 'Only men have real names in our society, women don't.' . . . He worried about his professional standing, colleagues trying to contact him—all kinds of things that women face as a matter of course when they get married....

"One of the things that came out in our discussion groups was that most of us had always been uncomfortable about sports. We knew we were *supposed* to be interested, and so we gradually fell into the pose. If you're an American male and don't recognize all the World Series players, you have little in common with other men— most of whom have learned all that stuff simply because it's expected of them . " (Jack Sawyer, in interviewed in New Woman, Feb. 1972, pp. 74 ff.)

To what extent do women contribute to forcing men into a masculine stereotype?

Was Jesus a liberated man?

How do men's liberation and women's liberation complement each other?

In The Executive's Wife, the author—herself both an executive and executive's wife—writes:

"Today, it is agreed, very few men reach the top brass classification unless their wives are socially acceptable. In fact, at the annual meeting of one of the country's most powerful corporations, the chairman of the board insists that the wife of each officer sit directly behind her husband. It is his public tribute to the invaluable performance of the distaff side." (Ninki Hart Burger, The Macmillan Company, 1968, p. 119.)

59

How does such an attitude affect a marital relationship?

How does it affect the choice of mate a man or woman makes?

What happens when a board officer has a husband instead of a wife?

Ralph Nader writes:

> "Our present retirement-security system is fragile at best, but particularly unfair to women. Our society encourages a woman, sometimes against her will, to stay home and take care of her family, and then penalizes her later for not having worked. Under the present law, a wife can receive only a portion of her husband's Social Security benefit if he dies. Widows are regularly excluded from pension benefits their husbands have earned." ("How You Lose Money by Being a Woman," *McCall's* Jan. 1972, p. 65.)

The Catholic Church has been one of the strongest forces in American society encouraging women not to take outside jobs. To what extent have we compensated women for their sacrifices?

Do we give them recognition for their talents? Do we protect them from financial need?

BIBLIOGRAPHY

"Male Lib," *NEW WOMAN* Magazine, Feb. 1972, p. 74.

A history of women from primitive religion up to the present, including sections on Hinduism, Buddhism, Confucianism and Islam. Very weak on contemporary Catholicism, but the best book on the overall picture.

A Mennonite view of the question.

A Room of One's Own by Virginia Woolf, Harcourt Brace Jovanovich, Inc.,© 1957.

Alice S. Rossi, "Equality Between the Sexes: An Immodest Proposal," from *The Woman in America*, ed. Robert Jay Lifton, Houghton Mifflin, Co.,© 1965.

Beard, Mary. Woman as Force in History. Collier, 1946.

Bird, Caroline. Born Female. D. McKay Company, 1968,

Burger, Ninki Hart. The Executive's Wife. Macmillan, 1968.

Callahan, Daniel. Abortion. Macmillan, 1970.

Callahan, Sidney Cornelia. The Working Mother. Macmillan, 1971.

Clemens, Lois Gunden. Woman Liberated. Herald Press, 1971.

Culver, Elsie Thomas. Women in the World of Religion. Doubleday, 1967,

Cunneen, Sally. Sex: Female; Religion: Catholic. Holt, Rinehart and Winston, 1968.

Daly, Mary. The Church and the Second Sex. Harper & Row, 1968.

Doely, Sarah Bentley, editor. Women's Liberation and the Church. Association Press, 1970.A first-rate collection of essays by leading Catholic and Protestant women. An excellent appendix includes such things as the report on "Sex Role Stereotyping in the United Methodist Nursery Curriculum."

Ellmann, Mary. Thinking About Women. Harcourt, Brace& World, 1968.

Ermarth, Margaret Sittler. Adam's Fractured Rib. Fortress, 1970.A Lutheran study of the role of women which includes summaries of what's going on in the other churches.

Figes, Eva. Patriarchal Attitudes. Stein and Day, 1970.

Flexner, Eleanor. Century of Struggle. Belknap Press, 1966.This is one of many fine histories of the woman suffrage movement in this country.

Friedan, Betty. The Feminine Mystique. Dell, 1963.

Gibson, Rev. Elsie. When the Minister is a Woman. Holt, Rinehart& Winston, 1970.The book has been sharply criticized by some Protestants as too 'unmilitant', but for Catholics unused to ordained women it can be quite helpful.

Gillespie, Dair. L. "Who Has the Power? The Marital Struggle." Journal of Marriage and the Family, August 1971, pp. 445-458.This entire special issue is devoted to "Sexism in Family Studies."

Granfield, David. The Abortion Decision. Doubleday, 1969.

Greer, Germaine. The Female Eunuch. McGrawHill, 1971.

Grisez, Germain. Abortion. Corpus, 1970.

Hellwig, Monika. "Hope and Liberation" Liturgy, Oct. 1970, pp. 13-15.This whole issue is devoted to the question of women in the church.

Her Infinite Variety by Morton M. Hunt, Harper & Row, Publishers, copyright © 1962, pp. 173-174.

Horner, Matina. "Fail: Bright Women." Psychology Today, Nov. 1969, pp. 36-38.

Hunt, Morton. Her Infinite Variety. Harper& Row, 1962.

Kanowitz, Leo. Women and the Law. University of New Mexico Press, 1969.

Lamson, Peggy. Few Are Chosen. Houghton Mifflin, 1968.

Malhas, Thurayya A.F. "The Moslem Arab Woman and Her Rights" Word, Nov. 1971, pp. 3-5.

Matina Horner, "Fail: Bright Women," *PSYCHOLOGY TODAY*, Nov. 1969, pp. 36-38. copyright © Communications/Research/Machines, Inc.

McKenna, Sister Mary Lawrence. Women of the Church. P.J. Kenedy, 1967.

Miller, Rev. Elizabeth. Retreat to Tokenism. Available from the Division of Christian Social Concern, American Baptist Convention, Valley Forge, Pa. 19581. 25c.A study of employment of Baptist women on the national level.

Millett, Kate. Sexual Politics. Doubleday, 1970.

Monika Hellwig, "Hope and Liberation," *LITURGY* (membership journal of the Liturgical Conference) Oct. 1970, p. 14.

Nader, Ralph. "How You Lose Money by Being a Woman." McCall's, Jan. 1972, pp. 65f.

Patriarchal Attitudes by Eva Figes, Stein & Day, Publishers,© 1970.

Presbyterian Life. Feb. 8, 1967. A complete issue devoted to the woman question.

Prof. Rosemary Ruether, "Are Women's Colleges Obsolete?" Reprinted from *THE CRITIC*, copyright © 1968 by the Thomas More Association, 180 N. Wabash Ave., Chicago, Illinois 60601.

Putnam, Emily James. The Lady. University of Chicago Press, 1970.

Ralph Nader, "How You Lose Money By Being A Woman," *McCALL'S*, Jan. 1972, p. 65.

Retreat to Tokenism by Rev. Elizabeth Miller, reprinted with permission of Division of Christian Social Concern, American Baptist Convention, Valley Forge, Pa.

Rev. Dr. Thomas Boslooper, printed in the *Times* on December 27, 1967. © 1967 by the New York Times Company. Reprinted by permission.

Rev. Elsie Gibson, *When the Minister Is a Woman*, Holt, Rinehart and Winston, Inc., 1970. pp. 70-71.

Rossi, Alice S., "Equality Between the Sexes: An Immodest Proposal." One of a number of interesting and intelligent articles in The Woman in America, edited by Robert Jay Lifton. Houghton Mifflin, 1965.

Ruether, Rosemary. "Are Women's Colleges Obsolete?" The Critic, Oct.-Nov. 1968, pp. 58-64.

Russell, Letty Mandeville. "Women's Liberation in a Biblical Perspective" Concern, May-June 1971. Available through YWCA. The entire issue of this Presbyterian magazine is a study guide for six discussion sessions.

Sawyer, Jack, interviewed by Arline Brecher."Male Lib" New Woman, Feb. 1972, pp. 72-ff.

Sixteen women write about their own experiences.

St. Anthony Messenger. March 1971.A whole issue devoted to women in the church with a number of significant articles and a series of short interviews.

Stendahl, Krister. The Bible and the Role of Women. Fortress, 1966.

Sweeney, Theodora Briggs. "Children, Church, and Lib." Word, Jan. 1971, pp. 18-19.

Swidler, Arlene. "Make Theology Your Business." Word, Dec. 1969, pp. 4-11.Jobs are scarcer now than when this was written, but it remains the only survey of theological opportunities for women.

Swidler, Leonard. "Jesus Was a Feminist." Catholic World, Jan. 1971, pp. 177-183.This study of the words and actions of Jesus as portrayed in the four gospels has been translated and reprinted in over a dozen countries.

The Executive's Wife by Ninki Hart Burger, Macmillan Co.,© 1968, p.119.

The Theory of the Leisure Class by Thorstein Veblen. All rights reserved. Reprinted by permission of The Viking Press, Inc.

This remains the best overall scholarly study of women in the Catholic Church.

Thurayya A.F. Malhas, "The Moslem Arab Woman and Her Rights," *WORD*, Nov., 1971, p. 3, National Council of Catholic Women.

Veblen, Thorstein. The Theory of the Leisure Class. Modern Library, 1934.

Woman Liberated by Lois Gunden Clemens. Copyright ©1971 by Herald Press, Scottdale, Pa. 15683.Reprinted by Permission.

Woolf, Virginia. A Room of One's Own. Harcourt, Brace, 1957.World Council of Churches Department on Cooperation of Men and Women in Church, Family and Society, Concerning the Ordination of Women. 1964.

Zborowski, Mark, and Elizabeth Herzog Life is with People. International Universities Press, 1952.A sociological study of the East European Jewish village, the shtetl, which includes interesting material on the attitude of Jews toward women.

Tell Us What You Think

We thank you in advance for taking a few minutes to give us your thoughts about this book. Authors look forward to receiving these comments. Please go here to share or email us at info@iPubCloud.com.

www.ingramcontent.com/pod-product-compliance
Lightning Source LLC
Chambersburg PA
CBHW050603280326
41933CB00011B/1967